60 DAYS OF
LOW·FAT
LOW·COST
MEALS
IN MINUTES

OVER 150 DELICIOUS,
HEALTHY RECIPES & MENUS
THAT FIT YOUR BUDGET

M.J. SMITH
R.D., M.A.

60 Days of Low-Fat, Low-Cost Meals in Minutes. ©1992 by
CHRONIMED Publishing, Inc.

Library of Congress Cataloging-in-Publication Data

Smith, M.J. (Margaret Jane), 1955-
   60 days of low-fat, low-cost meals in minutes : over
   150 delicious, healthy recipes & menus that fit your
   budget / M.J. Smith.
      p.   cm.
   Includes bibliographical references and index.
   ISBN 1-56561-010-5 : $12.95
   1. Low-fat diet—Recipes. 2. Menus. 3. Low budget cookery.
4. Quick and easy cookery. I. Title. II. Title: Sixty days of low-
fat, low-cost meals in minutes.
RM237.7.S58   1992   92-26421
641.5'638—dc20   CIP

Edited by: Susan Van Cleaf
Cover & Text Design: Terry Dugan Design
Art/Production Manager: Claire Lewis
Typesetting: Wordex, Lory Strom
Printed in the United States of America

Published by:
CHRONIMED Publishing, Inc.
P.O. Box 47945
Minneapolis, MN 55447-9727

TABLE OF CONTENTS

* * * * *

ACKNOWLEDGEMENTS

My sincere appreciation is extended to everyone who used my first book, to those who praised the pie they served at a holiday meal, and to those who suggested that the bean salad needed a little more garlic. Also thanks to my own clients and personal friends who kept bringing up new ideas and sharing new recipes. And lastly, thanks to my family and my registered dietitian buddies, who kept me going when the spatula got stuck in the mixer.

* * * * *

PREFACE

L *ow-fat* . . . the diet buzzword of the 90's.

Everyone seems to watch their dietary fat. And it's getting easier all the time. In fact, nutrient labels are boldly spelling out grams of fat, right on the fourth line.

But as a practicing dietitian, I know that people still are confused about fat. How many fat grams should I eat each day? How do I know that my menu has the right type of fat? How does a fast food meal fit into a low-fat diet? What about sugar? It has no fat, but can I eat too much? Amid the explosion of low-fat foods, which ones actually taste good?

I wrote this book as a follow-up to my first cookbook (*All American Low-Fat Meals in Minutes*). In this second book, I emphasize a 60-day plan for a low-fat diet, complete with shopping lists and preparation tips. First comes a primer on low-fat cooking and shopping, followed by menus and the 150 new recipes.

Readers frequently ask a cookbook author, "Where do you get your ideas?" Many recipes and menus were adapted from higher fat versions that I discovered in restaurants and magazines or from the hundreds of client diet histories that I analyze each year. My kitchen is my laboratory, and that is where I measure and evaluate low-fat ingredient substitutions and cooking method changes.

Too many low-fat recipes get all bogged down in "method," like the ones that say to "freeze a bowl of something until mounds heap." This book is different, because I threw out recipes if they weren't short on prep time and long on taste.

1

In fact, when clients come to my office for a low-fat diet, they are anxious for the simplest of advice, such as, "How do I grill white fish so that it tastes great and doesn't fall through the grate?"

So, that is what this second book is all about: 60 days of low-fat eating that is short on prep time, long on taste. Success with a low-fat diet still begins and ends with real food.

* * * * *

Why Is Everyone Watching Fat?

When I saw a recent story about how to count fat grams on "20/20," the ABC television news magazine, I cried "Hallelujah!" For years, dietitians have been telling people to actually measure out a teaspoon of margarine, choose skim-milk cheeses, and drain their ground beef in a colander. But, all of a sudden, counting fat grams is a national news story.

What's behind this surge of news media attention on watching fat content? For the first time, all of the major health organizations are reading off the same menu. Let me give you a run-down:

The American Heart Association—Its *Eating Plan for Healthy Americans* says, ". . . your goal will be to gradually reduce your fat intake to 30% (of total calories) or even slightly lower." This publication is written for all healthy Americans over the age of two and is intended to promote a wholesome eating style while reducing blood cholesterol to safe levels.

American Institute for Cancer Research—Its *Dietary Guidelines to Lower Cancer Risk* says, "How much fat people eat in their diets has been linked again and again to their chances of getting cancer. It seems to apply particularly to cancers of the breast, colon, rectum, ovary and prostate. Reduce the intake of total dietary fat . . . to no more than 30% of total calories and, in particular, reduce the intake of saturated fat." This publication makes a strong argument that you can lower your chances of getting cancer by eating smarter each day.

USDA—Its *Dietary Guidelines for Americans* says, "Choose a diet low in fat, saturated fat . . ." The government is in the business of telling us how to eat for a number of reasons, but one of the most critical is that our national health costs for lifestyle-induced diseases continues to spiral.

The American Academy of Family Physicians—
Its *Nutrition Strategies* says, "Limit the fat in your diet. Each gram of fat equals 9 calories . . . A fat-rich diet encourages weight gain . . . ." Family doctors continue to be the first to be approached when someone wants to reduce, and they are advising patients to cut total fat intake and exercise to lose weight.

Other major groups, including the American Diabetes Association are chiming in, and recent surveys indicate that 67% of Americans are hearing the message and are on regular low-fat diets today.

An exciting potential side effect of a low-fat diet is that it may be insurance against aging. Combining a low-fat diet with exercise to slow aging is a concept currently being studied by Dr. Roy Walford, of the University of Wisconsin, Madison, in the Biosphere 2 project. Dr. Walford's theory is that "undernutrition (restriction of fat and calories) without malnutrition" will retard aging and dramatically extend life span, even when such a regimen is started in adulthood.

I make no promise that the menus and recipes in this book will extend your life span to age 150, but they do tastefully fit all of the major health organizations' guidelines for controlling fat. **Thus, they are useful for lowering blood cholesterol and reducing cancer risk.** For a list of low-fat foods and specific instructions on counting fat grams for weight loss, see the next section.

* * * * *

THE LOW-FAT LIST

A quick and clean way to achieve a low-fat diet involves three principles:

1. Consume lean foods liberally: Fruits, vegetables, breads, starches and skim milk products.

2. Control portions of lean meats and unsaturated fats and oils.

3. Avoid saturated fats: Fat red meats, poultry skin, butter, cream, whole milk, solid shortening, coconut oil, cocoa butter, palm and palm kernel oil, hydrogenated fats.

The following food list, with suggested serving sizes, corresponds with these three principles.

Eat	**Avoid**
Fruits and Vegetables	
All in liberal amounts, *Aim for 5 servings daily.*	Olives, avocado and coconut Palm, coconut, palm kernel oils
Milk Products	
Skim, 1/2%, and 1% milk and foods made from them Cheese with 2 or fewer grams of fat per ounce Nonfat cottage cheese Nonfat yogurt *Aim for 2 servings daily.*	Whole and 2% milk, cream cheese with more than 2 grams of fat per ounce Nondairy creamers Regular and low-fat cottage cheese and yogurt

Eat	**Avoid**

Breads and Cereals

Plain breads and rolls	Egg, butter or cheese-rich
Low-fat crackers (for	breads
sample brands, check	Party crackers
index for page number	Potato and snack chips
of "Express Shopping")	Mixes for cakes,
Pretzels, breadsticks	breads, or cookies
Popcorn	Rice and pasta mixes
Cereals	with added fat
Rice and pasta	Chunky soup
Starchy vegetables	
Broth or skim milk	
based soups	
Aim for 6 servings daily.	

Meat, Fish, Poultry, Proteins

Skinless chicken and turkey	All poultry skin
Lean, trimmed red meats	Duck, goose
85% lean ground beef	Prime red meats
Packaged sandwich meats	Regular ground beef
with 2 grams of fat per	Pastrami, ribs
ounce	Rib eye cuts, hot dogs
Fish, except those packed	Sausage, bacon
in oil	Luncheon meats
Dried beans, peas, legumes	Bratwurst
Egg whites (limit yolks to	Organ meats
4 weekly)	
Wild game	
Limit all meat to 3 ounces per	
meal (same size as a deck of cards)	

Eat

Avoid

Fats and Oils

Limit intake of the following oils to 1-2 teaspoons per meal:
Canola or Rapeseed
Safflower
Sunflower
Corn
Soybean
Cottonseed
Sesame
Olive
Stick, tub or squeeze
  margarines made from
  those oils
Salad dressing made from
  those oils
Low calorie salad dressings
Peanut butter
Seeds and nuts in 1 TB. servings

All solid fats and shortening
Butter
Bacon fat
Ham hocks
Meat fat
Margarines that are not
  made from approved sources
Chocolate
Coconut
Coconut oil
Palm oil
Palm kernel oil

* * * * *

WEIGHT CONTROL ON A LOW-FAT DIET

A fter years of study on obesity and weight loss, dietitians have come to the conclusion that "dieting" simply doesn't work for the vast majority of people. While many initially succeed in shedding weight, the pounds often creep back, in many instances leaving the dieter heavier than they were to begin with.

Worse yet, there is growing consensus that repeated losses and gains — called "yo-yo dieting" — may actually heighten certain health risks.

In my 14 years of experience working with individuals toward long-term weight control, I have refined my approach many times and now use the following five simple guidelines:

1. Scale back expectations. This means looking at only 10- to 15-pound increments of weight loss. Even modest weight loss can produce positive changes in blood pressure, blood sugar and cholesterol levels. If you lose 15 pounds and keep it off for six months, then start in on the next 15.

2. Focus on health and the comforts of daily living instead of weight in pounds. The number on the scale can only take on the meaning you assign to it. But the flabby stuff around your middle translates directly into more work for your heart, how your clothes fit and how easily you can bend over to tie your shoe. Set your goals to correspond with these important health and daily living changes. Just being able to climb the basement steps without heavy breathing will give you a feeling of "winning."

3. Consider the "readiness factor." Certain times of the year will be good for you to initiate big-time diet and exercise changes. Simply recording your food intake will require 10 minutes a day. Look at your daily schedule over the next three months. Define exactly how and when you are going to fit "food record" into that schedule. For most people, November 15 is not a good time to start diet change. With the craziness of the holiday season just around the corner, few people can find the energy to sustain the commitment and motivation necessary for success.

4. To lose weight and keep it off, exercise is mandatory. Exercise is a requirement, and it is as simple as that. By elevating your heart rate during brisk walking or cycling, you are burning calories at a faster rate than normal, and you continue to burn calories at a fast rate for one to three hours after the activity is finished. Exercise also helps to build and maintain muscle mass. This is like money in the bank, because muscle tissue requires more calories than fat to be maintained. Burning calories to maintain muscle tissue is an on-going aid in long-term weight control. And let's face it, whether you are walking or working out to your aerobic dancing video, you are not eating! I suggest a minimum of three exercise sessions weekly, 45 minutes each, to reduce weight.

5. Eat a low-fat diet and record your food in terms of grams of fat. These are the guidelines that I use to promote gradual weight loss:

> For women to lose weight, limit fat to between 35 and 45 grams daily.

> For men to lose weight, limit fat to between 50 and 60 grams daily.

The guidelines suggested above promote a gradual weight loss, generally one-half to one pound per week. Weight loss is slow, and this means that long-held troublesome habits are more likely to be replaced by new healthy ones.

What about maintaining your weight? If you feel that your current weight is "healthy for you" and relatively easy to maintain, you can use these guidelines for counting grams of fat:

> For women to maintain weight, limit fat to between 50 and 60 grams daily.

For men to maintain weight, limit fat to between 60 and 70 grams daily.

Your activity level affects how much fat you can eat and still maintain your weight. The weight loss and weight maintenance guidelines are meant for someone exercising three times each week, for 45 minutes per session. This exercise may be walking or cycling or square dancing or swimming, or doing leg-lifts from your easy chair — any activity that gets you moving! I stress that there is no substitute for physical activity to promote heart health, retard aging, ward off osteoporosis and control weight.

The next section is a step-by-step lesson on recording fat grams in your diet.

How To Record Fat Grams

Writing down what you eat and counting the fat in grams from those foods is a proven and direct link to successful weight control. By writing down: "1 c. orange juice — 0 gm. fat, 1 c. skim milk — 1 gm. fat, 1 bran muffin — 5 gm. fat, 1 tsp. margarine — 5 gm. fat," you learn quickly that doing without margarine cuts breakfast fat in half. A hidden benefit of this important practice of food recording is that you will make many small discoveries about reducing fat in your own favorite foods and menus.

Turn now to the "Pocket Guide to Fat Grams" in the next section. Notice that the grams of fat in fruits, vegetables, skim milk products, and grains are very low, while the fat grams in red meats, margarines, and oils add up quickly. This Pocket Guide listing of fat represents the average amount of fat for that food group, and you can use the numbers for many plain food items. To count grams of fat from brand name processed and prepared foods, as well as from fast food restaurants, you must purchase a food counter book. I would recommend Corrine Netzer's *The Complete Book of Food Counts*. It is available for $6.95 (includes shipping) from Dell Readers Service, Department DCN, P.O. Box 5057, Des Plaines, Illinois 60017. Ask for order number 20062 - 8. This food counter book lists plain foods, as well as name brand processed and prepared foods, in common serving sizes. Analysis of fat grams also is provided for all of the menus and recipes you'll be using in this book.

Counting fat grams allows you to pick and choose how you want to spend your "fat allowance" for the day. It is very important that the fats you choose in your daily allowance come from desirable sources, the mono- and polyunsaturated fats. *Simply aim to avoid the saturated fats: fat and marbling in red meats, poultry skin, butter, cream, and whole milk, products made from cream and whole milk, solid shortening, coconut oil, cocoa butter, palm and palm kernel oil, and hydrogenated fats.*

Here is an example of counting fat grams for a day:

Keeping Track of Fat Grams		Date 2/3/92
Food/Amount	Fat, grams	Calories
1 c. cream of wheat	2	160
2 slices toast	2	160
1 tsp. margarine	5	45
1 c. coffee	0	0
1 c. tea	0	0
1 orange	0	60
3 oz. white chicken	3	165
1 baked potato	1	80
1 Diet Coke	0	0
3 oz. lean burger	12	165
½ c. mashed potato	1	80
1 c. snap peas	0	50
1 c. skim milk	1	90
1 home baked chocolate chip cookie	7	100
Totals:	34	1155

My fat allowance is 40 grams daily.

If you are aiming for 25% to 30% of your total calories from fat, you can check yourself. To calculate the percentage of calories from fat, multiply grams of fat by 9, then divide by the total calories. Look at this example:

Grams of fat __34__

_____ x 9 calories per gram

__306__ calories from fat

Divide calories from fat by total calories and multiply the answer by 100 to find out the percentage of calories from fat.

$$306 \div 1155 = .26$$
$$.26 \times 100 = 26\% \text{ of calories from fat.}$$

Photocopy the blank form shown below for your own use.

Keeping Track of Fat Grams	Date	
Food/Amount	Fat, grams	Calories
Totals:		

My fat allowance is _____ grams daily.

To calculate percentage of calories from fat, multiply grams of fat by 9, then divide by the total calories. Multiply the answer by 100.

Pocket Guide to Fat Grams

The following guide can be used for estimating intake of fat. Numbers reflect averages for the food group.

Food	Fat (grams)
Nonfat beverages, 1 cup serving, including coffee, tea, mineral water, fruit juices, fruit drinks, tomato and vegetable juice, and sugar-free soft drinks	0
All fruits, 1/2 cup serving	0
Vegetables, 1 cup serving, including aspara- gus, beets, broccoli, carrots, cauliflower, celery, cabbage, cucumber, eggplant, green or yellow beans, lettuce, mushrooms, onions, peas, radishes, Brussels sprouts, kohlrabi, leeks, okra, pea pods, spinach, sauerkraut, zucchini, and water chestnuts	0
Starchy vegetables, 1/2 cup serving including potatoes, corn, squash, baked beans, lima beans, sweet potatoes and yams	0
Dairy products	
2% milk, 1 c.	5
1% milk, 1 c.	3
Skim or nonfat milk, 1 c.	0
Low-fat cottage cheese, 1/2 c.	3
Nonfat cottage cheese, 1/2 c.	1
Low-fat yogurt	5
Nonfat yogurt	1
American cheese, 1 oz.	9
Cheddar cheese, 1 oz.	9
Swiss cheese, 1 oz.	8
Part-skim cheese, 1 oz.	2-5
Ice cream, 1/2 c.	7
Sherbet, 1/2 c.	0
Ice milk, 1/2 c.	3
Sorbet, 1/2 c.	0
Frozen yogurt, 1/2 c.	3

Food	*Fat (grams)*
Grains and cereals, including:	
Any cereal without nuts, 1/2 c.	1
Rice, pasta or barley, 1/2 c.	
Bread, buns, English muffin or bagel, 1 slice	
Soda crackers or rye-crisps, 4 squares	
Pretzels or breadsticks, 1 oz.	
Angel food cake, 1 slice	
Vanilla wafers, 2	
Meats, 1 oz. cooked serving	
Poultry, white meat, no skin	1
Poultry, dark meat, no skin	2
Fish, any white fish, tuna or salmon	1
Beef, including chuck, flank, rib-eye,	4
round, lean ground beef, top loin, T-bone	
Must be lean and well-trimmed	
Pork including chop, loin or shoulder, or	4
very lean ham. Must be lean and well	
trimmed.	
Egg, 1 whole	5
Fats and Oils	5
Hard margarine or vegetable oil, 1 tsp.	
Diet margarine, 2 tsp.	
Mayonnaise or peanut butter, 2 tsp.	
Salad dressings (oil variety), 1 TB.	
Seeds or nuts, 1 TB.	

Add your favorite foods below:

_____

_____

_____

_____

_____

_____

_____

My fat allowance is _____ grams daily. Use this guide when recording daily fat grams.

* * * * *

WHAT ABOUT SUGAR, SALT AND ALCOHOL?

I *s too much sugar dangerous?*

This question has come to the forefront as dietary intake has shifted away from fatty foods. The short answer to this question is that moderate amounts of sugar are safe.

Now, for the qualifiers. Sugar is still concentrated in calories. So, you shouldn't add scoops of the white stuff to your Cream of Wheat® or strawberries, if you are watching calories for weight control. Sugar does not contribute any essential nutrients, such as vitamins and minerals, so it should not play a prominent role in your total intake. Sugar also contributes to tooth decay. For people with high triglycerides (a type of blood fat), restricting sugar is a part of the dietary treatment. There are other troublesome effects of sugar, including its relationship to reactive hypoglycemia (low blood sugar).

But as long as sugar is used wisely, it can be a part of a healthy diet. Sugar has many functions, besides providing for a naturally sweet taste. For instance, it aids the browning reaction in baked items. This is why you will see it in moderate amounts in certain recipes in this book.

Can this book can be used successfully by people with diabetes?

The recipes and menus have been developed using the 1986 Exchange System, with permission from the American Diabetes Association and the American Dietetic Association. See the reference chart that follows:

Exchange* List	Carbohydrate gms.	Protein gms.	Fat gms.	Calories
Starch/Bread	15	3	trace	80
Lean Meat	-	7	3	55
Vegetable	5	2	-	25
Fruit	15	-	-	60
Skim Milk	12	8	trace	90
Fat	-	-	5	45

When possible, sugar substitutes have been tested and recommended for use with recipes. If a recipe did not lend itself satisfactorily to using a sugar substitute, none is mentioned.

Persons with diabetes or hypoglycemia should not have foods containing large amounts of regular sugar. This warning has been added to some desserts in this book, including Pavlova (which is a meringue shell with a fruit filling). This warning about sugar is most significant for persons with diabetes using insulin. On the other hand, single servings of low sugar desserts at the end of the meal may be acceptable. Persons with diabetes should check with their physician or dietitian about the use of low-sugar desserts as part of their meal plan.

* The Exchange Lists are the basis of a meal-planning system designed by a committee of the American Diabetes Association and the American Dietetic Association. While designed primarily for people with diabetes and others who must follow special diets, the Exchange Lists are based on principles of good eating that apply to everyone. *Exchange Lists for Meal Planning,* copyright 1989, is published by the American Diabetes Association and the American Dietetic Association.

Is sodium reduced in the menus and recipes?

My approach is to "tastefully reduce sodium." This means low-sodium foods, such as no-added-salt tomato juice and crackers with unsalted tops, are included on the menus. Sodium-containing ingredients (such as salt, soy sauce, and baking soda) are limited or omitted in the recipes, as long as the final product tastes good. The average amount of sodium in the daily menus is 3 grams or 3000 milligrams, and this is in keeping with guidelines for blood pressure control. Three grams of sodium is the equivalent of 1 1/4 teaspoons of table salt.

Can alcohol be part of a healthy diet?

The answer to this question has everything to do with amounts. You will notice that, on the weekend menus, I have included a light beer or a wine cooler. Many dietitians and physicians have recommended alcohol in moderation. What this translates into is one or two servings, and they cannot be all saved up for Saturday night. A serving is considered to be 12 ounces of beer, 5 ounces of wine or 1 1/2 ounces of liquor. Some studies suggest one drink a day raises the "good" HDL cholesterol, and this can be considered a health benefit. Drinking alcoholic beverages in larger amounts depresses and displaces other beverages, such as milk or fruit juice, that are rich in nutrients. Of course, pregnant and nursing women and persons using medicines incompatible with alcohol should avoid using beer, wine or spirits.

* * * * *

KITCHEN BASICS FOR THE LOW-FAT COOK

Get organized! Here are ten tips for getting out of the kitchen:

1. Organize your kitchen to eliminate unnecessary steps. Keep staples in one place. Set up one cupboard to store all your baking supplies. Stow your everyday utensils together in an easy-to-reach place. Keep spices and seasonings in alphabetical order.

2. Fight clutter. Garage sale those appliances and cookware that you haven't used in two years.

3. Stop messes before they happen. Line cookie sheets and broiler pans with foil for easy washing. Coat pans with nonstick cooking spray.

4. Plan ahead. Always double casserole recipes. Eat one that day and freeze the second in an oven-proof dish for later on.

5. Wash and dry all of your salad greens at once. They will store easily in a covered container in the refrigerator.

6. Delegate. Everyone who enjoys the meal deserves to help in its creation. Three-year-old children can help set the table and sixty-year-old men can help clear it.

7. Invest in a slow-cooker. Many lean meats need long moist cooking to tenderize. What's nicer than coming home to a meal that's ready when you are?

8. Put your food processor or mini-chopper to work. It will be faster (even considering the clean-up) than hand chopping. Keep other kitchen utensils in good repair. Sharpen knives, replace worn spatulas and repair loose handles on cookware.

9. Keep a running grocery list in a handy place. If you run out of raisins or light bulbs, jot it down immediately.

10. Begin tomorrow's menu today. Before shutting off the lights in the kitchen, have one or two steps on the next day's menu completed.

Kids in the Kitchen

Research shows that children who participate planning family meals have healthier eating styles as adults, accept a wider variety of foods and conduct themselves politely in company. Here's how to get them started:

1. Include their favorites on the weekly menu.

2. Ask children as young as three to help set the table.

3. Start by washing hands with soap and water. Keep the trash can and damp sponge nearby for easy cleanup.

4. Introduce children to the microwave with an easy task, such as reheating leftovers or making hot cocoa.

5. Stress organization. Give children their own work space to use and to clean up.

6. Work through recipes step by step.

7. Let the kids hand-stir the quick bread or muffin batter as you add the liquid ingredients.

Shortcut to Food Measurement

Take the guesswork out of measuring with these equivalents:

Food, measurement	Equivalent
Almonds, whole, 1 lb.	3 cups, chopped
Apples, 1 medium	1 cup, sliced
Bananas, 1 medium	1/2 cup, mashed
Beans, dry, 2 1/2 cups (1 lb.)	6 cups, cooked
Bread, 1 slice	1/4 cup dry, fine crumbs
Bread, 1 slice	3/4 cups soft crumbs
Cabbage, 1 small (1 lb.)	5 cups, shredded
Carrots, 7 medium (1 lb.)	2 1/2 cups, chopped
Carrots, 7 medium (1 lb.)	3 cups, shredded
Celery, 1 medium bunch	4 cups, chopped
Cheese, 4 oz.	1 cup, shredded
Cranberries, 4 cups (1 lb.)	3 cups sauce
Eggs, 8 whites	1 cup
Graham crackers, 16 squares	1 cup crumbs
Green beans, 3 cups (1 lb.)	3 cups, cooked
Lemons, 1 medium	3 TB. juice, 2 tsp. peel
Limes, 1 medium	2 TB juice, 1 1/2 tsp. peel
Macaroni, 1 cup, uncooked	2 cups, cooked
Meat, boneless, 1 lb., raw	2 cups, chopped, cooked
Mushrooms, 6 cups (1 lb.), fresh	2 cups, sliced, cooked
Onions, 1 medium	1/2 cup, chopped
Noodles, 3 cups, uncooked (4 oz.)	3 1/2 cups, cooked
Oranges, 1 medium	1/3 cup juice, 4 tsp. peel
Peaches, pears, 1 medium	1/2 cup, sliced
Peppers, 1 large	1 cup, chopped
Popcorn, 1/4 cup, unpopped	5 cups, popped
Potatoes, 1 medium	1/2 cup, mashed
Potatoes, 1 medium	2/3 cup, cubed
Rice, long grain, 1 cup, uncooked	3 cups, cooked
Rice, quick, 1 cup, uncooked	2 cups, cooked
Soda crackers, 28 crackers	1 cup crumbs
Spaghetti, 8 oz., uncooked	4 cups, cooked
Spinach, 20 cups (1 lb.)	2 3/4 cups, cooked
Strawberries, whole, 4 cups	3 1/2 cups, sliced
Tomatoes, 1 medium	1/2 cup, cooked
Vanilla wafers, 22 wafers	1 cup crumbs

Suitable Substitutes

Food	Substitute
Baking powder, 1 tsp.	1/2 tsp. cream of tartar plus 1/4 tsp. baking soda
Buttermilk, 1 cup	1 cup plain yogurt
Buttermilk, 1 cup	1 TB. lemon juice or vinegar with milk to make 1 cup
Cayenne pepper, 1/8 tsp.	4 drops liquid hot red pepper seasoning
Cornstarch, 1 TB. for thickening	2 TB. flour
Flour, self-rising, 1 cup	1 cup flour plus 1 1/4 tsp. baking powder, 1/8 tsp. salt
Garlic, minced, 1 clove	1/4 tsp. garlic powder
Honey or corn syrup, 1 cup	1 1/4 cups sugar plus 1/3 cup liquid
Molasses, 1 cup	1 cup honey
Mustard, prepared, 1 TB.	1/2 tsp. dry mustard plus 2 tsp. vinegar
Onion, 1 small chopped	1 TB. dried minced onion
Sugar, 1 cup	1 cup packed brown sugar
Sugar, 1 cup	2 cups sifted, powdered sugar
Tapioca, quick-cooking, 2 tsp.	1 TB. flour
Wine, red, 1/2 cup	1/2 cup grape juice
Wine, white, 1/2 cup	1/2 cup apple juice

Using 50% Reduced Fat Margarines

Fifty percent reduced fat margarine (such as Promise Light™ or Mazola Light™) works wells as a substitute for regular margarine, in the same amounts, for sauteing vegetables. Since water has been added to these margarines, they do not always substitute successfully for regular margarine in bread and dessert recipes.

Meat and Poultry Cooking Chart

Frozen Beef Steaks

Beef Cut, 1 in. Thick	Inches from Heat	Cooking Time in Minutes	
		Rare (140° F.)	Medium (160° F.)
Rib Eye	5	19	24
Top Loin	5	19	24
Tenderloin	5	17	22
Top Sirloin	5	27	32

Fresh Beef Steaks

Beef Cut, 1 in. Thick	Inches from Heat	Cooking Time in Minutes	
		Rare (140° F.)	Medium (160° F.)
Rib Eye	3 - 4	10	15
Top Loin	3 - 4	12	17
Tenderloin	3 - 4	10	15
Top Sirloin	3 - 4	16	21

Roasting Beef

Cut, Doneness, Weight in Pounds	Final Meat Temperature	Cooking Time, Minutes per Pound
Sirloin, rare, 8 - 12	120° - 125°	16 - 20
Sirloin, medium, 8 - 12	145° - 150°	20 - 22
Sirloin, well, 8 - 12	155° - 165°	26 - 30
Sirloin Tip, rare, 3 - 5	120° - 125°	28 - 30
Sirloin Tip, medium, 3-5	145° - 150°	34 - 38
Sirloin Tip, well, 3 - 5	155° - 165°	40 - 45
Rump, rare, 5 - 7	120° - 125°	20 - 22
Rump, medium, 5 - 7	145° - 150°	26 - 28
Rump, well, 5 - 7	155° - 165°	29 - 32
Rolled Rump, 4 - 6	155° - 165°	35 - 38
Top Round, rare, 3 - 6	120° - 125°	28 - 30
Top Round, medium, 3 - 6	145° - 150°	34 - 38
Top Round, well, 3 - 6	155° - 165°	40 - 45
Rib Eye, rare, 3 - 6	120° - 125°	12
Rib Eye, medium, 3 - 6	145° - 150°	16
Rib Eye, well, 3 - 6	155° - 165°	18 - 20

Pork

Thickness / Weight	Final Meat Temperature	Cooking Time, Minutes per Pound
America's Cut, broiled		
1 in.	170°	11 - 13
1 1/2 in.	170°	18 - 20
Bone-In Loin Chop, broiled		
3/4 in.	170°	12 - 14
1 1/2 in.	170°	23 - 25
Chef's Prime, roasted		
2 - 4 lb.	170°	28 - 33
Top Leg Roast, roasted		
3 1/2 lb.	170°	38 - 42
Ground Pork Loaf, roasted in 425° F. oven		
1 - 1 1/2 lb.	170°	55 - 65

Poultry Roasting

Bird / Weight in Pounds	Oven Temperature	Final Meat Temperature	Cooking Time in Hours
Chicken, 2	400°	190°	1 - 1 1/2
Chicken, 3 - 4	375°	190°	1 1/2 - 2 1/4
Chicken, 5 - 9	325°	190°	3 - 5
Chicken, halves	400°	190°	3/4 - 1
Turkey, 4 - 8	325°	185°	1 3/4 - 2 3/4
Turkey, 8 - 12	325°	185°	3 1/2 - 4
Turkey, 12 - 16	325°	185°	4 - 4 1/2
Turkey, 16 - 20	325°	185°	4 1/2 - 5
Turkey, 20 - 24	325°	185°	5 - 6
Turkey Breast, 2 - 4	350°	185°	1-1 3/4
Turkey Breast, 4 - 6	350°	185°	1 3/4 - 2 1/4
Turkey Breast, 6 - 8	350°	185°	2 1/4 - 3 1/4
Turkey Breast, 8 - 10	350°	185°	2 3/4 - 3 1/4
Cornish Hen, 3/4 - 1 1/2	350°	180°	3/4 - 1 1/4

Poultry, Broiling

Bird / Weight for Broiling	Distance from Heat	Cooking Time on Each Side
Chicken, 3 - 5 lb.	6 in.	20
Turkey, 4 - 6 lb.	9 in.	30

How To Cut Up and Bone a Chicken

Skinless, boneless chicken is a staple on a low-fat diet. For economy's sake, you may want to buy a whole chicken and cut it up yourself. Follow these steps:

1. Cut the skin between the body and thighs. Bend the legs until the bones break at the hip joints.

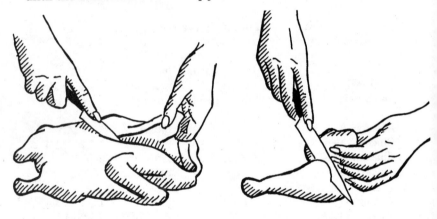

2. Remove the leg and thigh pieces from the body, by cutting with a sharp knife between the hip joints as close to the backbone as possible.

3. Separate the thighs and leg, by first cutting through the skin at the knee joint. Break the joint, then cut the thigh and leg apart.

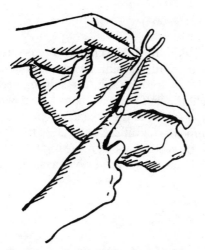

4.   To remove the wings from the body, cut through the skin on the inside of the wings at the joint. Break the joint, then cut the wings from the body.

5.   Divide the body. Cut along the breast end of the ribs to the neck to separate the breast and back sections. Bend the back piece in half to break it at the joint. Cut through the broken joint. Cut off the tail, if desired.

6.   Divide the breast into two lengthwise pieces, by cutting along the breastbone.

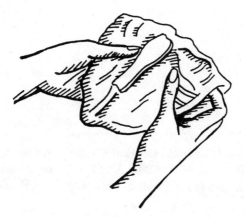

To skin and bone the breast:

First remove the skin. Place the chicken breast on a cutting board, skin side up. Pull the skin away from the meat and discard. Use a heavy knife to split the chicken breast in half, lengthwise. Hold the half of breast bone side down. Starting from the breastbone side of the breast, cut meat away from the bone, using a thin sharp knife. Cut as close to the bone as possible. Continue cutting, using a sawing motion. Press the flat side of the knife blade against the rib bones. As you cut, gently pull meat up and away from the bones.

From *The New Doubleday Cookbook* by Jean Anderson and Elaine Hanna. Copyright 1985. Used with permission of Doubleday, a division of Bantam Doubleday Dell Publishing Group, Inc.

Never Failing with Fish

Why do even accomplished cooks shy away from preparing fish? Even if you've had a flop with fish in the past, don't make a big deal out of something simple. Follow these tips for never failing.

Buying fish: High-quality whole fish should have red gills, and light pink to red flesh. Flesh should be elastic, yet firm. Fillets and steaks should have a firm fresh appearance. Avoid pieces with a strong odor, dried edges or dull, slimy skin. Frozen fish should be solidly frozen, and the sides of a block of fish should be straight, not curved in or out. The package should show no signs of frost and should be tightly sealed. Store fresh fish immediately in moisture-proof material in the refrigerator, and use as soon as possible.

Broiled fish: For best results with broiling, use thawed fish. Place fillets or steaks in a single layer on a greased, unheated rack in a broiler pan. Tuck under any thin edges. Dot with low-fat margarine (allow 2 teaspoons per fillet). Then season with your favorite flavoring agents. Salt, pepper, lemon pepper, finely grated lemon peel, dill weed, thyme, basil, or cajun seasoning all work well. Broil fish 4 inches from the heat, until fish flakes easily when tested. Allow 10 minutes.

To test any fish for doneness: Insert fork into the fish at a 45 degree angle. Twist the fork gently. If fish resists flaking and is still translucent, it is not done. If it flakes apart easily and is milky white, it is done. A dry and mealy texture is a sign of over-cooked fish.

Baking frozen fillets: Allow frozen block of fish to thaw in the refrigerator long enough so that it can be cut with a knife. Cut into portions and place in a greased shallow baking pan. Dot with reduced calorie margarine (allow 2 teaspoons per fillet). Season. Bake uncovered in a 450° oven for 25 to 30 minutes or until it tests done.

Baking thawed fillets: Cut into portions, place on pan, dot with reduced calorie margarine and season as directed above. Bake uncovered in a 450° oven, allowing 5 to 6 minutes for each 1/2 inch of thickness. Test for doneness.

Micro-cooking fish: Cut frozen fish into portions and place in a greased, nonmetal baking dish. To thaw, cover with waxed paper, then microwave on high power for 2 minutes. Let stand for 2 minutes. Turn fish over and give the dish a one-quarter turn. Cook 1 minute on high power and let stand 2 minutes. Again give the dish a one-quarter turn. Cook 1 minute on high power and let stand 2 minutes. Then microwave 30 seconds. Dot the thawed fish with reduced-calorie margarine and season as directed above. Cook on high power for 7 to 8 minutes, or until the fish tests done. Give the dish a half-turn after 4 minutes.

A Primer on Dried Beans and Lentils

Types of Beans:

Black—Black skinned, creamy flesh. Staple of South American soups.

Black-eyed—Southern favorites. Flavor resembles field peas.

Cannellini—White Italian kidney beans. Good with tomato dishes.

Chick-peas—Also called garbonzo beans. Are nut-like and work well in soups, salads and casseroles.

Fava—Wrinkled, beige in color and strong in flavor. Known for their large size.

Kidney—Familiar, reddish-brown color. Used in chili and Mexican dishes.

Lima—Baby limas are light green and have a delicate flavor.

Pinto—Similar to kidney bean, but freckled.

Red beans—Smaller, redder variety of kidney beans.

White—Family of beans that includes the great northern and navy varieties.

To prepare beans for cooking, place them in a colander or large sieve and rinse them well in cool water. Sort carefully, removing withered or broken beans. Soak using basic or quick method:

Basic soaking—Allowing 1 quart of cold water for each pound of dried beans, soak overnight or for 6 to 8 hours.

Quick soaking—Allowing 1 quart of cold water for each pound of dried beans, place beans and water in a large kettle, cover and bring to a boil. Reduce heat to medium and allow to boil gently for 2 minutes. Remove from heat. Let stand for 1 hour with the lid on.

To cook beans, use some of the soaking water, because nutrients are present. Do not add salt or any acidic ingredients (such as tomatoes) until the end of the cooking time. To keep the bean pot from boiling over, add 1 teaspoon of oil or margarine to the liquid.

Lentils and Split Peas:

Lentils and split peas are members of the legume family. They are much smaller than their bean cousins and do not require soaking before cooking.

To cook these small legumes, rinse and drain them. Use twice the amount of water as split peas or lentils. Do not add salt or any acidic ingredients. In a saucepan, combine split peas or lentils with water. Cover, bring to a boil, and then reduce to a simmer. Continue simmering for 15 minutes for salads, 30 minutes for main dishes, 45 minutes for soups.

For persons bothered by gas from dried beans and lentils, there is a helpful product called "Beano." It is a solution containing a natural enzyme that breaks down the hard-to-digest carbohydrates in gassy foods. "Beano" should be available in most pharmacies.

Guide to Selection of First Rate Produce

Apples—Select those with good color and a fresh bright and shiny appearance. Apples should be firm to the touch. Refrigerate.

Apricots—Pick plump, fairly firm, golden-yellow apricots. They last up to three weeks in the refrigerator.

Artichokes—Choose compact, heavy, plump artichokes. They should be green with some color variations.

Avocado—While very high in fat, avocados can garnish a Mexican meal. Fresh avocados should be free from bruises, have even coloring and be slightly soft to the touch. Ripen at room temperature.

Bell Peppers—Red or green peppers should be firm and glossy, free of spots.

Broccoli—Choose green or purplish-green broccoli. Look for full flowered tops on a short stem.

Brussels Sprouts—Shop for firm, compact sprouts with good green color.

Cabbage—For best quality, choose a heavy compact head without signs of discoloration. To decrease the aroma of cooking cabbage, drop a whole walnut into the cooking water.

Cantaloupe—Look for cantaloupes with a slightly golden under-color and netting that stands out prominently. Touch the stem end, and it should feel slightly soft when ripe. A ripe melon gives off a sweet aroma.

Carrots—Carrots should be firm and bright orange. If they become soft or wilted, they can be crisped up in cold water.

Cauliflower—Look for white color and heavy firm body. Refrigerate. Before using, place it head down in cold water, with a teaspoon of vinegar and 1/4 teaspoon salt. This will crisp it and draw out any insects.

Celery—Crunchy celery is most delicious when selected for crisp, clean stalks that are thick and solid. Color should be medium to bright green.

Iceberg Lettuce—Best quality lettuce has a springy-firm feeling when pressed by the fingers. Core, rinse and thoroughly drain lettuce before storing in an airtight container in the refrigerator.

Kale—Look for fresh and young heads. Avoid those with coarse stems and dry or yellowing leaves. Younger leaves are tender and can be used for salads. Older and larger leaves are suited for cooking. A sprinkling of vinegar enhances the kale's flavor.

Kiwifruit—Kiwifruit should be about the same firmness as pears, slightly soft to the firm touch. Avoid any with soft spots or indentations. Kiwifruit are not suited to gelatin salads, as they have an enzyme that interferes with setting of gelatin.

Kohlrabi—The bulb and top of this vegetable are edible. Select smaller kohlrabi for delicate flavor.

Onion—Avoid buying onions that are crackly, dry or soft, or have spots from sunburn, mold or decay. Store in a cool, dry place.

Orange—Oranges should feel heavy, be evenly bright orange, slightly shiny and soft to the firm touch.

Papaya—A mostly green papaya will ripen in 5 to 7 days at room temperature. Keep ripe papaya in the refrigerator for one week.

Potato—Potatoes should be firm and smooth. Avoid those with wrinkled or wilted skins or soft dark areas. Store in a cool, dark, well-ventilated place.

Spinach—Spinach leaves should appear crisp, not soft or wilted. Look for deep green even color.

Strawberry—Select berries that are firm, dry, plump and fully colored, with the cap stem attached. Eat within a few days after purchase.

Sweet Potato—Quality sweet potatoes will be thick and chunky and will taper toward the end. Do not refrigerate.

Tomato—Supermarket tomatoes are seldom fully ripe. Place in a ventilated paper bag and store at room temperature to ripen.

Watermelon—First check for a dry, brown stem and bright green color. Then thump with the knuckles. The sound should be deep and hollow.

Winter Squash—Acorn and butternut squash should be selected for their smooth, hard rind. Lightweight squash may be dry and stringy. These will store from 30 to 50 days.

Microwave Tips

The microwave oven is a low-fat cook's best friend. The fastest way to discover its benefits is to use it—with all kinds of recipes. The recipes in this book have been tested with an Amana Radarange™ with 700 watts of cooking power. If your microwave unit has different cooking power, you will need to adjust the cooking time accordingly. If you are having less than fantastic results with your microwave, review the checklist below for sure-fire success.

1. Use the utensils recommended in the recipe. The size, shape and material of the utensil are all important. Large size dishes often are suggested because they guard against boil-overs. Glass covers (rather than paper towels or no cover at all) tend to reduce cooking time by retaining moisture. If you don't have a glass lid for the dish, substitute heavy-duty plastic wrap that has been pierced with a 1-inch slit. Remove any cover slowly away from you to avoid steam burns.

2. Use the cooking time recommended. Often a range is given, such as 15 to 18 minutes. Check the product at 15 minutes. If it is not finished cooking, add another minute, check at 16 minutes and so on. Low-fat foods generally require longer cooking times than similar high-fat versions, because fat is a good heat conductor.

3.   If you double a recipe, multiply the cooking time by 1.75 (just slightly less than twice as long). Likewise, if you are cutting a recipe in half, multiply the cooking time by .6 (slightly more than half the time).

> Example:
> 15 minutes cooking time
> Double the recipe—15 min. x 1.75 = 26.25 min.
> Half the recipe—15 min. x .6 = 9.00 min.

4.   Food usually is placed on the oven floor. Because microwaves enter the oven cavity from the bottom, foods cook the fastest if placed there. If you have a rack for your unit, use it for delicate recipes that cannot be stirred, such as lasagne. Most recipes will be improved by rotating the product at least once during cooking. The food near the outside of the dish cooks fastest. Place the thickest part of the food toward the outside, rather than near the middle of the container.

5.   When preparing a meal with several microwave-cooked items, sequencing becomes important. Prepare the items with longest cooking time first, such as casseroles or sauces. If these items are covered, they will retain their heat. Foods that require short cooking times (such as fish or steamed fresh vegetables) should be cooked very close to serving. Foods that are simply being reheated or warmed (such as a basket of rolls) should be done last.

Cutting Fat From Your Own Favorite Recipes

You may be a bit squeamish about modifying old favorite family recipes, but my experience has shown that these low-fat substitutions are very subtle.

If recipe calls for,	*use these instead,*	*and save*
Bacon, 2 strips	1 oz. Canadian bacon	8 gms. fat
Baking mix, 1 cup	1 cup "light" baking mix	8 gms. fat
Beef, regular ground, 1 lb.	1 lb. 90% lean ground beef	44 gms. fat
Cheese, cheddar, 1 oz.	1 oz. part-skim cheddar	7 gms. fat
Cheese, cottage, 1/2 cup	1/2 cup nonfat cottage cheese	5 gms. fat
Cheese, cream, 1 oz.	1 oz. 50% fat cream cheese	5 gms. fat
Cheese, ricotta, 1/2 cup	1/2 cup part-skim ricotta	7 gms. fat
Cheese, shredded, 1 cup	1 cup shredded part-skim mozzarella	28 gms. fat
Chicken, 1 breast	1 skinless chicken breast	7 gms. fat
Chocolate, baking, 1 oz.	3 TB. cocoa and 1 TB. vegetable oil	4 gms. fat
Cream, heavy, 1 cup	1 cup evaporated skim milk	89 gms. fat
Cream, sour, 1 cup	1 cup 50% fat sour cream	20 gms. fat
Cream, sour, 1 cup	1 cup nonfat plain yogurt	40 gms. fat
Egg, 1 whole	2 egg whites	5 gms. fat
Half and half, 1 cup	1 cup evaporated skim milk	26 gms. fat
Ice cream, 1 cup	1 cup ice milk	6 gms. fat
Margarine, 4 TB. in pasta, stuffing, and rice mixes	1 TB. margarine and 3 TB. bouillon	36 gms. fat
Mayonnaise, 1 TB.	1 TB. 50% fat mayonnaise	6 gms. fat
Milk, evaporated, 1 cup	1 cup evaporated skim milk	18 gms. fat
Milk, whole, 1 cup	1 cup skim milk	9 gms. fat
Oil, 2 TB. for sauteing	1 TB. oil and 1 TB. bouillon, or water, or nonstick cooking spray	12 gms. fat / 24 gms. fat
Sausage, Italian, 1 lb.	1 lb. 90% lean ground beef with 2 TB. Italian seasoning	162 gms.fat
Soup, creamed, 1 can	1 recipe "Mary's Creamed Soup Substitute" (see page 190)	16 gms. fat
Steak, sirloin, 1 lb.	1 lb. sirloin steak, well-trimmed	37 gms. fat

* * * * *

EXPRESS SHOPPING FOR LOW-FAT FOODS

T
he inventory of food products on the next several pages will help you select high-quality low-fat products at your favorite market. This handy guide should complement the weekly shopping lists. For instance, if the shopping list calls for no-oil salad dressing or reduced fat mayonnaise, you can look at the inventory of salad dressings and find several brands to try. These foods and brand names, where listed, are recommended based on their favorable ingredients as well as acceptable taste.

If you are equipping your kitchen with low-fat cooking staples for the first time, review the "Staples" section on the weekly shopping lists and get started by buying those items.

Deli Case

Lean roast beef
Ham and turkey ham
Turkey and chicken breast
Part-skim farmer's cheese
Part-skim mozzarella
Breadsticks
Submarine buns
Hard rolls
Rye, French and Italian bread
Pita and sandwich pockets
Triple bean salad
Jello with fruit
Cranberry-orange relish
Copper penny salad
Pickled cauliflower
Corn relish
Diet chef's salad
Diet tossed salad
Dressing with chicken meat
Baked beans
Chicken to go (no skin)
Barbecued beef
Spaghetti
Chili
Beef stew
Chop suey
Almond chicken
Cheese pizzas
Soups: Vegetable beef, bean,
  vegetable chowder and
  chicken noodle
Vegetable relish tray
Fruit tray
Deluxe meat tray

Bread and Bakery

Plain breads, rolls, buns
Croutons, Wasa bread
Angel food cake
Breadsticks and English muffins
Bagels
French and rye bread

Meat, Fish and Poultry

Sirloin sandwich steak
Plain catfish
Minute steaks
Sirloin steaks
90% lean ground beef
Ground round
Ground chuck
Pork loin chop
Pork sirloin cutlet
Pork rump roast
Canadian bacon
95% lean ham
All chicken (remove skin)
Tyson skinless chicken
Louis Rich turkey breast
Louis Rich ground turkey
Longmont turkey ham
Whole turkey
Turkey breast
Raw shrimp and scallops
Crab legs and lobster tail
All unbreaded fish fillets
Rabbit
Beef or turkey burgers
Louis Rich turkey sausage
Louis Rich frankfurters
Land O Frost chicken
Louis Rich turkey ham
Louis Rich white chicken
Any 95% lean sliced ham

Produce

All fresh fruits
All fresh vegetables,
    except avocados
Potatoes and other tubers
Dried fruits
Marie's Lite Salad Dressings

Salad Dressings and Condiments

Miracle Whip Free
Weight Watchers Salad Dressings
Hellman's nonfat mayonnaise
Kraft Free Dressings
Light Western Dressing
Henri's Light Dressings
Seven Seas Free Dressings
Take Heart Dressings
Marzetti Fat Free Dressing
Richard Simons Spray
Estee Dressing Mixes
Kraft Oil Free Dressings
Henri's Less Oil Dressings
Hudson Bay Croutons
Cooking wines
Bacon bits
Vinegars
Pickles
Mustard and ketchup
Dill mustard
Worcestershire sauce
Mrs. Dash Steak Sauce
La Choy Lite Soy Sauce
La Choy Lite Teriyaki Sauce
Lawry's Fajita Mix

Canned Fruits and Vegetables

Any canned fruit in juice
Del Monte Fruit Naturals
Libby's Lite Fruit in Juice
All fruit juices
All canned vegetables
Pork and beans (remove fat cube)
All vegetable juices

Chinese and Mexican Foods

Soy sauce
Teriyaki sauce
Water chestnuts
Chow mein noodles
La Choy Classic Dinners
Fortune cookies
Taco sauce
Taco shells and mini taco shells
Garbanzo beans
Taco seasoning

Canned Meats

White chunky chicken
Premium white chicken
Any tuna packed in water
Salmon
Sardines in water or
    tomato sauce
Herring, clams and oysters

Pasta and Legumes

All eggless pasta
Dried beans, peas, lentils
Dried bean soup mix
Tomato sauce and paste
Ragu Fino Italian Sauce
Prego Extra Chunky Sauce

Packaged Dinners and Side Dishes

Limit margarine to 1 TB.:
    Rice a Roni
    Suzi Wan rice dishes
    Lipton rice and sauce
    Stuffing mixes

Near East dishes
Barley
Minute Rice
Long grain and wild rice
Frank-O-American Spaghetti
   (no meat)
Cheese pizza mixes
Rice and popcorn cakes
Ragu Chicken Tonight
   Oriental and Salsa flavors

Frozen Foods

Plain frozen vegetables
International vegetables
Birdseye Custom Cuisine
Chow mein vegetables
Microwave vegetables
Pict Sweet Express
Healthy Choice dinners
Le Menu Lite Style:
   Turkey Divan
   Chicken Cacciatore
   Herb Roasted Chicken
Lean Cuisine:
   Chicken Marsala
   Glazed Chicken with
      Vegetables
   Turkey Breast
Weight Watchers:
   Chicken Fajitas
   London Broil
All fruit juices and drinks
Pillsbury Microwave Pancakes
Aunt Jemima Pancakes
Belgian Chef Waffles
Aunt Jemima French Toast
Kelloggs NutraGrain Waffles
Microwave Super Pretzels
Tombstone or Totino's Pizza:
   Cheese and Canadian Bacon
Whole fruits
Rhodes bread dough
English muffins and bagels

Ice milk
Frozen yogurt:
   low-fat and nonfat varieties
Ice milk bars and Fudgesicles
Sherbet and sorbet
Kemps Juice Koolers
Crystal Light Bars
Jello Pops
Kemps Lite Fudge Jr's
   Sugar Free Fudgesicles
Kemps Lite Assorted Pops

Refrigerator and Dairy Products

Fruit juices and drinks
Whole fruit products
Vegetable juices
Egg substitutes
English muffins and bagels
Skim and 1% milk
Light 1/2% milk
Light sour cream
Nonfat or 1% cottage cheese
Ricotta part-skim cheese
All 1% or nonfat yogurt
Butter Buds
All stick, tub, squeeze, or
   diet margarines made from
   safflower, sunflower, corn,
   cottonseed, canola, sesame,
   olive or partially hydrogen-
   ated soybean oil
   Look for a P/S radio of 2/1.
Choose these tub margarines:
   Fleischmann's, Mazola,
   Weight Watchers and
   Promise
Light Philadelphia Cream Cheese
Kraft Spreadery Cheese
Kraft Light Singles
Borden's Lightline Cheese
Light 'n Lively Cheese
Trimline Cheese Product
Part-skim mozzarella cheese

Mootown Snackers String Cheese
Weight Watchers Cheeses
Light and Natural Kraft Cheese
Fresh fettucini and angel hair pasta
Corn and flour tortillas

Staples, Seasonings, Baking and Dessert Items

Flours and cornmeal
Spices, seasonings and salt
Molly McButter
Mrs. Dash Crispy Coating
Pam and No-Stick
Sugar and substitutes
All gelatin products
Pudding mixes
  (make with skim milk)
Angel food and chiffon cake
Pillsbury Lovin' Lite mixes
Duncan Hines DeLights mixes
Royal Light cheesecake
Bisquick Light baking mix
Pie fillings and solid pumpkin
Cocoa and yeast
Jelly, jam and honey
Maple and corn syrups
Hungry Jack Pancake Mix
  (make with skim milk)
Carnation Cocoa Mix
Dry and evaporated skim milk
All coffee and tea

Breakfast Cereals and Products

Carnation Instant Breakfast
Chewy Granola Bars
Shark Bites and Fun Fruits
Fruit Wrinkles and Rollups
Nature Valley Bar
Quaker Chewy Granola Bar
Oatmeal and all oat cereals
  except Cracklin' Oat Bran
Quaker Whole Wheat

Maltex, Ralston, Maypo,
  Maltomeal and grits
All types of muesli (no nuts)
All bran cereals (no nuts)
All corn and rice cereals
Grape Nuts
All wheat cereals
Puffed rice and wheat

Cookies

Archway:
  Date Filled Oatmeal
  Gingersnap
  Oatmeal Raisin
Frookies
Keebler Playland
Vanilla wafers
Animal crackers
Pepperidge Farm:
  Ginger and Molasses
Fig Newtons

Crackers and Soups

Knorr and Lipton soup mixes
Mrs. Grass soup mixes
Soup starters and bouillon
Progresso broth and vegetable
  soups
Campbell's soups:
  broth-based and
  Healthy Request
All Health Valley soups
Hilton's chowders
Soda and oyster crackers
Graham crackers
Thin Bits
Wheatables
Jacobsen's Toast
Wasa Extra Crisp
Ak-Mak Original Crackers
Devon Melba Crackers
Crackle Snax
Rye and Oatbran Crisp

Snacks and Soda

Orville Redenbacher's
   Light Microwave Popcorn
Pop Secret Light Popcorn
Any whole popping corn
Confetti popcorn
Pretzels
Limit to 1 oz. serving:
   Combos and Chex Snack Mix
   Doritos Light Chips
All sodas and bottled waters
Beer, wine and spirits as
   directed by your doctor

Kitchen Gadgets That Cut the Fat

Metal or plastic strainer—to drain ground beef
No-stick skillet—to minimize need for oil
No-stick loaf and muffin pans—for baked goods
No-stick baking sheet—for baking fish
No-stick saucepan—for sauces and soups
Cutting board—for slicing vegetables
Grater—for grating carrots and part-skim cheeses
Microwave casserole dishes—for freeze and thaw
Salad bowl with cover—for salads that keep
Steamer—for bright tender crisp vegetables
Wire whisk—to make smooth sauces
Salad spinner—to wash and store fresh greens
Wooden spoons—for no-stick surfaces
Pastry brush—for light coats of oil
Egg separator—to use just the whites
Mini-Chopper—for chopping vegetables
Roasting pan and grate—to keep meat out of fat
Vessel with low spout—for de-fatting broth
Pepper mill—for fresh ground taste
Measuring cups and spoons
Spatula, slotted spoon, and ladle
Pasta portioner
Kitchen scissors
Kitchen scale
Upright poultry roasting rack
Screen grill—for fish

A Low-Fat Cook's Christmas Wish List

Automatic bread baker
Wok
Gas grill
No-stick cookware set, such as Scanpan, Farberware, or T-Fal
Wide toaster for bagels and muffins
Expresso/cappuccino maker
Juicerator

Kitchen Gadget Catalogs

Colonial Garden Kitchens
P.O. Box 66
Hanover, PA 17333-0066
Call 1-800-7525-552 to request a catalog

Williams-Sonoma
P.O. Box 7456
San Francisco, CA 94120-7456
Call 1-415-421-4242 to request a catalog

The Chef's Catalog
3215 Commercial Ave.
Northbrook, IL 60062-1900
Call 1-800-338-3232 to request a catalog

Crate and Barrel
P.O. Box 9059
Wheeling, IL 60090-9059
Call 1-800-323-5461 to request a catalog

King Arthur Flour
Baker's Catalogue
R.R. 2, Box 56
Norwich, Vermont 05055
Call 1-800-827-6836

The Art of Food
Community Kitchens
P.O. Box 23121, Dept. HW
Baton Rouge, LA 70821-2311
Call 1-800-321-7539

* * * * *

WHAT'S THE BIG DEAL ABOUT MENU PLANNING?

When I ask my clients, "Do you plan your menus?," most of them get flustered and sputter something like, "Well, sort of." Effective low-fat menu planning doesn't mean a seven-course dinner on white linens. Rather, the planning itself and the express shopping for low-fat foods are the critical factors for success with a low-fat diet. If you have no low-fat plan, the quick-grab, high-fat choices will get in the way of your being in control.

You'll see that the menus in this book are based upon a lean protein source, two servings of breads or cereals, a large helping of vegetables, some fruit and skim milk. It is just that simple. In this section of the book, I have organized my know-how about menus to help you easily adopt a low-fat diet. The canny hints, lucky discoveries and practical advice in this section on menus are meant to be read and digested slowly! You cannot change everything overnight. Some readers will want to pick up the 60 days of low-fat menus and follow them to the letter. That's great! But just as many will peruse the ideas and then pluck out the ones that will jive with their schedules and tastes.

Three Squares A Day Plus Snacks

I still believe in three meals a day. There has been a lot of talk about "grazing" in the last five years. A whole generation seems to love to eat on the run, in front of the TV, in the car, at the mall, on the phone or over the newspaper at the kitchen counter. My argument for three regular meals has to do with the "fullness factor." If you eat a low-fat breakfast containing some protein, you aren't going to feel honest-to-goodness hunger again until close to lunch time. Same goes for a noon meal. If you plan a low-fat lunch with plenty of fiber and protein, you can resist that late afternoon urge to splurge.

45

This doesn't mean that low-fat snacks between meals are out. Since the fat content of food is what makes you feel full, expect to want "a little something" two or three hours after eating a low-fat meal. I have included a whole section on low-fat snacks to make your choices informed ones.

Another important reason for sitting down to eat is the subconscious message that says "you are eating a meal." You tend to honestly forget about food after you have enjoyed a meal at the table. Eating on the run does not send this same message to the brain. Instead, the message sent is, "I am in a hurry. I am doing two things at once."

Breakfasts

Eating breakfast just makes sense. It is the meal that refuels your body after 10 or 12 hours of fasting; it starts you on your way—wherever you're headed. The famous "Iowa Breakfast Studies," conducted in the 1950's confirmed that kids did better in school when they had eaten breakfast. Also, a whole bunch of "big kids" out there watching their fat intake would do better today if they were following that landmark advice. A recent study, entitled "The American Breakfast Report," showed that persons eating a simple breakfast of cereal and milk consumed fewer total calories during the day and fewer calories from fat.

The breakfast menus that follow are samples of plans that fit the low-fat diet prescription. Menus for the weekends are more elaborate, because everyone loves a "Big Sunday Breakfast."

Lunches

I want to chuckle at clients who tell me about their "light lunches" . . . "just one trip to the salad bar." By the time I chalk up all the fat grams from those "light salads," I need an adding machine with a paper tape. Food trends show that most of us do eat lunch away from home—in restaurants with friends or co-workers, in cars with fast-food carry-outs, at desks with leftovers from the night before, or in workplace cafeterias. The low-fat lunch menus I have included cover all of these bases, plus eating lunch at home.

Dinner

Dinner is the "big meal of the day." Research shows that about five nights a week, it will be at home. And dinner has to be quick—even at home. We would rather be doing things other than slaving in the kitchen, so the dinner menus that follow are extra speedy through the week. Saturday and Sunday have some extra fancy touches, because our pace usually is more relaxed. Notice the "Do Ahead" list for each day. Don't miss the "Go Meatless" menus. You'll even find out what to do with leftovers.

Managing Leftovers

In the weekly menus, at least one dinner is set aside for "Fast-Food Pickup or Cleaning out the Refrigerator." Everybody has leftovers now and then, and they can be a welcome sight as you arrive home after a hectic day. You also can work in leftover breads or fruits at breakfast, or you can warm up leftover casseroles, entrees or vegetables for lunch the next day.

Exchange Diets

If you are using the daily menus as part of an exchange diet, the
meal patterns represented by the menus are shown below:

Food Groups	Number of Exchanges		
	1200 calories (33 gms. fat)	1500 calories (42 gms. fat)	1800 calories (50 gms. fat)
Breakfast			
Fruit	1	1	1
Bread/Starch	2	2	2
Fat	1/2	1	1
Skim milk	1	1	1
Lunch			
Lean meat	2	3	3
Bread/starch	1	2	2
Vegetable	2	2	2
Fruit	1	1	2
Fat	1/2	1	1
Skim milk	—	—	—
Dinner			
Lean meat	2	3	3
Bread/starch	1	2	3
Vegetable	2	2	2
Fruit	1	1	2
Fat	1/2	1	2
Skim Milk	1	1	1
Add snacks worth	125 calories 5 gms. fat	125 calories 5 gms. fat	150 calories 5 gms. fat

Where Do I Go From Here?

60 Days of Menus

What follows next are 60 days of menus. Breakfast and lunch menus are included for the first two weeks. Beginning in Week 3, you can write in your own breakfast and lunch menu ideas. Now we're "taking the training wheels off," and you are on your own. Go back to Weeks 1 and 2 for ideas. The nine *Week-at-a-Glance* menus feature corresponding shopping lists. The *Day-at-a-Glance* menus come after the shopping lists and include serving sizes for three different calorie and fat levels. The daily menus are for those who want tight control on their fat and calorie intake. When a menu item is preceded by an asterisk (*), the recipe is included in this book. Check the index for the page number.

All of the daily menus instruct you to choose something from the "Grab-A-Snack" list (check index for page number). You'll find that a low-fat meal leaves you hungry two or three hours after eating. It's OK! When you reduce fat in the diet, you also change the feeling of fullness you get from food. When true hunger strikes, just choose a snack that also is low in fat from the many ideas listed.

Easy ways to increase the ability of meals to satisfy you are to use 1% milk instead of skim or to add 1 teaspoon of reduced-fat margarine. Remember that both techniques add a few fat grams to the meal.

WEEK-AT-A-GLANCE MENUS AND SHOPPING LISTS
Week 1 Full Day Menus At-A-Glance

Breakfast	Lunch	Dinner	Snacks	Do Ahead:
Monday				
Choice of Fruit	Stacked Thin-Sliced	*Fajitas with Iowa	Choices from	Start salad for
Juice	Lean Ham on left-over	Beef	Grab a Low-Fat	Tuesday lunch.
*Breakfast in the Car	French Bread with	Lettuce and Tomatoes	Snack List	Start double
Skim Milk	Mustard	*Pina Colada Fruit		recipe of soup
Coffee or Tea	Light Potato Chips	Salad		(Tuesday/
	Fresh Veggies	Skim Milk		Wednesday).
	Green Grapes			
	Iced Tea			
Tuesday				
Grape Juice	*Greek Tuna and	*Hamburger Soup	Choices from	Thaw chicken
Choice of Hot Cereal	Salad	Soda Crackers	Grab a Low-Fat	breasts for
Toasted Bagel	Leftover Bagel	*Crunchy Broccoli	Snack List	Wednesday
Low-Fat Margarine	Raisins	Salad		dinner.
Jam	Mineral Water	Canned Tropical Fruit		
Skim Milk		Blend in Juice		
Coffee or Tea		Skim Milk		
Wednesday				
Choice of Juice	Leftover Hamburger	Grilled Chicken Breast	Choices from	Make muffins for
Bran Cereal	Soup	on a Hamburger Bun	Grab a Low-Fat	Thursday
Fresh Berries	Soda Crackers	Lettuce and Tomato	Snack List	breakfast.
Wheat Toast	Fresh Orange	Corn on the Cob or		
Low-Fat Margarine	Diet Soft Drink	Whole Kernel Corn		
Skim Milk		Low-Fat Margarine		
Coffee or Tea		Fresh Pineapple		
		Skim Milk		
Thursday				
Orange Juice	Leftover Chicken Breast	*Spanish Pork Chops	Choices from	Start salad for
*Banana Breakfast	on Wheat Bread	with Peppers	Grab a Low-Fat	Friday lunch.
Muffin	with Mustard,	Baked Potato	Snack List	
Oatmeal with Raisins	Lettuce and Pickles	Corn Muffin		
Skim Milk	Light Potato Chips	Low-Fat Margarine		
Coffee or Tea	Fresh Apple	*Cabbage Salad with		
	Hot Tea	Poppy Seed Dressing		
		Sliced kiwifruit		
		Skim Milk		
Friday				
Low-Fat Yogurt	*Creole Shrimp Salad	FAST FOOD PICKUP	Add your choices from	Start raisin
Piece of Fresh Fruit	Leftover Corn Muffin	Check out suggestions	Grab a Low-Fat	bread, pot-
Toast with Low-Fat	Cranberry Juice	from your favorite	Snack List	atoes, cookies
Margarine or a		drive-through or		and dip for
Leftover Muffin		CLEAN OUT THE		Saturday.
Skim Milk		REFRIGERATOR		
Coffee or Tea				
Saturday				
Choice of Juice	*Football Saturday	*Potato, Green Bean	Choices from	Prepare break-
*Sportsman's Breakfast	Couch Potatoes	and Bacon Supper	Grab a Low-Fat	fast pie and
*Crunchy Raisin Bread	*Hot Broccoli Dip	Salad	Snack List	cake. Start
Skim Milk	with Fresh Vegetable	*Beer and Cheese		soup for
Coffee or Tea	and French Bread	Biscuits		Sunday.
	Dippers	*Snickerdoodles		
	Light Beer	Skim Milk		
Sunday				
Cranberry Juice	*Chicken Gumbo	*Beef Burgundy in a	Choices from	Start chicken
*Overnight Breakfast	Hard Rolls with Low-	French Bread	Grab a Low-Fat	salad, bean
Pie	Fat Margarine	Crust	Snack List	casserole and
*Cranapple Breakfast	*Old Fashioned	*Sweet and Sour		strawberry
Cake	Cucumber Salad	Bean Salad		salad for
Skim Milk	Sherbet	*Glazed Pineapple		Monday.
Flavored Coffee	Iced Tea	Skim Milk		

*See Day-at-a-Glance Menus for Serving Sizes

SHOPPING LIST FOR WEEK 1 FULL DAY MENUS

Take this book along to your supermarket or photocopy the list!
Select the same number or size of items that you have in the past, based on the number of people for whom you are shopping. Specific amounts of major ingredients in feature recipes are listed. Review this list before you go to the store. Cross out items that you have on hand and from those meals that you'll be eating away from home. Write in your personal likes and needs.

Produce
4 cups fresh fruit for breakfast pitas and pina colada salad
Grapes
Lettuce (2 meals)
Tomatoes (3 meals)
Fresh berries
Oranges
Pineapple (2 meals)
Apples
Potatoes (2 meals)
Kiwifruit
4 green or red peppers
Scallions
1 large bunch broccoli
Red onion
Celery
16 oz. mushrooms
Carrots
Bananas
8 new potatoes
1 1/2 lb. green beans
1 lb. shredded cabbage
Parsley
1 lemon
4 cups cucumbers

Bottled/Canned
Jam or jelly
Tropical fruit in juice
Pineapple juice
2 cans 6 1/2 oz. tuna in water
Reduced calorie herb vinaigrette dressing
4 cans 14 oz. chunky tomatoes
Sliced pineapple in juice
1/2 cup picante sauce
8 oz. whole cranberry sauce
4 cups chicken broth
15 oz. can kidney or garbanzo beans
Apple juice
1/2 cup chicken broth

Packaged
Hot cereal of choice
Raisins
Soda crackers
Bran cereal
Pickles for sandwiches
Corn muffin mix
Orzo or choice of pasta
6 cups light baking mix
3 cups quick rice
Corn flake crumbs
Bread crumbs
Oatmeal
Coconut

Staples/Spices
Salt
Pepper
Coffee or tea
Walnuts
Prepared mustard
Lime juice
Fresh garlic or garlic powder
Rum extract
Coconut cream (optional)
Low-fat or nonfat mayonnaise
Sugar or substitute
White vinegar
Basil
Dill weed
Celery salt
Cinnamon
Dry mustard
Poppy seeds
Red wine vinegar
Honey
Celery seed
Bay leaf
Worcestershire sauce
Flour
Brown sugar
Baking powder

Oregano
Rosemary
Powdered sugar
Filé powder (optional)
Thyme
Hot pepper sauce

Meat Case
Chicken breasts for grilling (2 meals)
1/2 lb. sirloin
1 lb. lean ground beef
4 pork chops, well trimmed
2 cups chicken pieces for making soup
1 lb. stew meat

Refrigerator Case
Skim milk
Low-fat margarine
Reduced fat cream cheese
Low-fat banana yogurt (2 meals)
4 flour tortillas
8 oz. plain nonfat yogurt
Part-skim mozzarella cheese
2 oz. feta cheese
8 strips bacon
Eggs or substitute
English muffins
Reduced fat Swiss cheese
Part-skim string cheese
Low-fat soft cheddar cheese spread
Part-skim cheddar cheese
2 cups low-fat cottage cheese

Frozen Case
Orange juice concentrate
Grape juice concentrate
Cranberry juice concentrate
Pita pockets
Corn on the cob
Sherbet
1 lb. salad shrimp
16 oz. broccoli
16 oz. hash browns
10 oz. okra
1 lb. bread dough

Other
Reduced fat potato chips (such as Ruffles Light)
Mineral water
Sugar-free soft drinks
Light beer
1/2 cup dry white wine
3/4 cup burgundy wine
Cream sherry

Bakery/Deli
Lean ham (need for 5 different meals during the week)
French bread (2 meals)
Bagels
Wheat bread
Hamburger buns
Hard rolls
Round loaf of rye bread

Non-Food Items/ Detergents/ Cleaning Supplies

Paper/Health/ Beauty

Week 2 Full Day Menus At-A-Glance

Breakfast	Lunch	Dinner	Snacks	Do Ahead

Monday
Crunchy Flaked Cereal
Fresh Banana
Wheat Toast
Low-Fat Margarine
Jam
Skim Milk
Coffee or Tea
	*Not Just Another
	  Chicken Salad
	Leftover Hard Rolls
	Low-Fat Margarine
	Leftover Pineapple
	  (from Sunday)
	Mineral Water
		GO MEATLESS
		*Bean Casserole
		  Ole'
		Light Corn Chips
		*Alison's Strawberry
		  Salad
		Skim Milk
		Coffee or Tea
			Choices from
			Grab a Low-Fat
			Snack List
				Thaw fish for
				Tuesday.
				Make muffins for
				Tuesday break-
				fast.

Tuesday
*Just Peachy Muffin
Cottage Cheese with
  Fresh Fruit
Skim Milk
Coffee or Tea
	Leftover Bean Casserole
	Leftover Light Corn
	  Chips
	Red Grapes
	Sugar-Free Soft Drink
		*Stuffed Sole
		*Italian Vegetable
		  Medley
		Sherbet
		Skim Milk
			Choices from
			Grab a Low-Fat
			Snack List
				Take the night
				off!

Wednesday
Apple Juice
Oatmeal
Leftover Muffin or
  Toasted Bagel with
  Low-Fat Margarine
Jam
Skim Milk
Coffee or Tea
	Peanut Butter and
	  Jelly Sandwich
	Low-Fat Fruited
	  Yogurt
	Sparkling Fruit Juice
		FAST FOOD PICKUP
		Check out suggestions
		from your favorite
		drive-through or
		CLEAN OUT THE
		REFRIGERATOR.
			Add your choices from
			Grab a Low-Fat
			Snack List
				Start scones.
				Start turkey
				salad and soup
				for Thursday.

Thursday
Choice of Juice
*Breakfast Scones
Jam
Part-skim String Cheese
Fresh Fruit
Skim Milk
Coffee or Tea
	*Turkey and Vege-
	  table Salad
	Low-Fat Wheat
	  Crackers
	Fresh Pear
	Iced Tea
		*Beefy Mushroom
		  and Barley Soup
		French Bread
		Low-Fat Margarine
		Cherry Tomatoes
		Ice Milk
		Skim Milk
			Choices from
			Grab a Low-Fat
			Snack List
				Start fondue for
				Friday.

Friday
Fresh Grapefruit
Scrambled Egg
Toast
Low-Fat Margarine
Jam
Skim Milk
Coffee or Tea
	Leftover Beefy Mush-
	  room and Barley Soup
	Soda Crackers
	String Cheese
	Tropical Fruit Juice
		GO MEATLESS
		*Friday Night
		  Fondue with Raw
		  Vegetables and
		  Tortilla Dippers
		*Red and Green Pea
		  Salad
		Wine Cooler
			Choices from
			Grab a Low-Fat
			Snack List
				Start raisin
				bread. Prepare
				and refrigerate
				grits casserole
				for Saturday.

Saturday
*Low-Fat Pancakes
  or French Toast
Applesauce with
  Maple Flavoring
Skim Milk
Coffee or Tea
	*Salmon and Pasta
	  Salad
	*Crunchy Raisin Bread
	Fresh Orange Slices
	Mineral Water
		*Hot Berry Wine
		*Broiled Ham with
		  Orange Glaze
		*Discover Grits
		  Casserole
		Green Salad with
		  Low-Fat Dressing
		*Cereal Pie Crust
		  with fruit filling
		Skim Milk
			Choices from
			Grab a Low-Fat
			Snack List
				Start quiche and
				lemon ring for
				Sunday.

Sunday
Orange-Pineapple Juice
*Quiche without the
  Crust
*Lemon Breakfast Ring
Skim Milk
Flavored Coffee
	Read the Sunday Paper
	  Lunch
	Sliced Turkey Rolled
	  with Toothpicks
	Low-Fat Wheat
	  Crackers
	String Cheese
	Green Apple Slices
	Grape Juice
		*Jambalaya
		French Bread
		Low-Fat Margarine
		Green Salad with
		  Low-Fat Dressing
		Sliced Fresh Pine-
		  apple
		Skim Milk
			Choices from
			Grab a Low-Fat
			Snack List
				Thaw chops for
				Monday.

*See Day-at-a-Glance Menus for Serving Sizes

SHOPPING LIST FOR WEEK 2 FULL DAY MENUS

Take this book along to your supermarket or photocopy the list!
Select the same number or size of items that you have in the past, based on the number of people for whom you are shopping. Specific amounts of major ingredients in feature recipes are listed. Review this list before you go to the store. Cross out items that you have on hand and from those meals that you'll be eating away from home. Write in your personal likes and needs.

Produce
Bananas
Fresh fruit for 2
  breakfasts
Red grapes (2 meals)
Pears
Cherry tomatoes
  (2 meals)
Grapefruit
Oranges
Salad greens (3 meals)
Granny Smith apples
Pineapple
1 1/2 cups celery
1 cup scallions
Onions
Green pepper
  (3 meals)
1/2 cup chopped
  peaches
1 lb. mushrooms
2 zucchini
2 yellow squash
2 tomatoes
4 large red-skinned
  potatoes
1 lb. green beans
1 red onion
1 large cucumber
1 lemon
Parsley
Raw veggies for
  dipping

Bottled/Canned
Jam or jelly
Tropical fruit juice
Applesauce (2 meals)
Reduced calorie or no-
  oil salad dressing
1/3 cup picante sauce
Low-fat or nonfat
  mayonnaise
2 cans 15 oz. pinto
  beans
14 oz. chunky
  tomatoes
8 oz. crushed
  pineapple
Apple

Quick barley
Green chili peppers
Reduced calorie Italian
  dressing
Reduced calorie
  cucumber dressing
Cran-raspberry juice
2 cans 15 oz. pink
  salmon
Pimento

Packaged
Flaked bran cereal
Coffee or tea
Choice of hot cereal
Low-fat wheat
  crackers
Soda crackers
1/2 cup almonds
Plain gelatin
3 cups light baking
  mix
Currants or raisins
Orzo pasta
Rotele pasta
1 1/4 cup quick grits
1/2 cup corn flake
  crumbs
Dry yeast
Oatmeal
Coconut
Parmesan cheese

Staples/Spices
Salt
Pepper
Peanut butter
Maple flavoring
Honey
Chili powder
Fresh garlic or garlic
  powder
Dried jalapeno
  pepper (optional)
Brown sugar
Cinnamon
Flour
Sugar
Baking powder
Vegetable oil

Lemon juice
Marjoram
Paprika
Basil
Chives
Celery seed
Dry mustard
White pepper
Worcestershire
  sauce
Cumin
Vanilla
Stick cinnamon
Whole cloves
Cider vinegar
Ginger

Meat Case
1 cup chicken to be
  cooked for
  chicken salad
2 cups turkey to be
  cooked for salad
1 lb. stew meat
1 lb. lean ham,
  sliced into 4 slices

Refrigerator Case
Skim milk
Low-fat margarine
Low-fat cottage
  cheese
Apple juice
  concentrate
Low-fat yogurt
Part-skim string
  cheese (3 meals)
Eggs or liquid
  substitute
Orange-pineapple
  juice concentrate
Grape juice
10 strips bacon
Part-skim
  American cheese
Part-skim
  Monterey Jack
  cheese
2 cups plain low-fat
  yogurt

1/2 cup buttermilk
Flour tortillas
1/2 cup soft cheddar
  cheese spread
Reduced fat Swiss
  cheese

Frozen Case
Sherbet
Ice milk
10 oz. strawberries
1 lb. sole, cod or
  orange roughy
Orange juice
  concentrate
16 oz. green peas
Grape juice
  concentrate

Other
Cream sherry
Mineral water
Light corn chips
  (such as Doritos
  Light)
Sugar-free soft
  drinks
Sparkling fruit juice
Wine cooler
1 qt. Burgundy
  wine

Bakery/Deli
Wheat bread
Hard roles (2 meals)
Sliced turkey (2
  meals)
French bread (2
  meals)

Non-Food Items
Detergents/
Cleaning Supplies

Paper/Health/
Beauty

Week 3 Dinner Menus At-A-Glance.
Write in Your Own Breakfast and Lunch Ideas!

Breakfast	Lunch	Dinner	Snacks	Do Ahead
Monday		*Honey Mustard Pork Chops Baked Potato Low-Fat Margarine Steamed Broccoli Wheat Dinner Roll Melon Balls Skim Milk	Choices from Grab a Low-Fat Snack List	Assemble casserole for Tuesday.
Tuesday		GO MEATLESS *End-Of-The-Month Vegetable Casserole Rye Bread Low-Fat Margarine Red Cherries Skim Milk	Choices from Grab a Low-Fat Snack List	Thaw tuna. May prepare relish for Wednesday.
Wednesday		*Grilled Tuna Steaks with *Vegetable Relish Wheat Rolls Low-Fat Margarine Orange and Grapefruit Sections Skim Milk	Choices from Grab a Low-Fat Snack List	Bake bread and start soup for Thursday.
Thursday		*Mulligatawney Soup Soda Crackers *Aloha Loaf Fresh Strawberries Skim Milk	Choices from Grab a Low-Fat Snack List	Relax!
Friday		FAST FOOD PICKUP Check out suggestions from your favorite drive-through or CLEAN OUT THE REFRIGERATOR.	Add your choices from Grab a Low-Fat Snack List	Start chili. May bake bread and cookies for Saturday.
Saturday		*Chicken Chili without Tomatoes *Dr. Downey's Whole Grain Bread Low-Fat Margarine Fresh Relishes *Carrot Cookies Light Beer	Choices from Grab a Low-Fat Snack List	Thaw roast. Start potatoes. May bake cake for Sunday.
Sunday		*You Can Microwave Pork Roast *Tipsy Sweet Potatoes Tomatoes and Cucumbers sprinkled with Vinegar, Sugar or Substitute and Dill Weed *Chocolate Cherry Cake with Vanilla Ice Milk on Top Skim Milk	Choices from Grab a Low-Fat Snack List	Relax!

*See Day-at-a-Glance Menus for Serving Sizes

SHOPPING LIST FOR WEEK 3 DINNER MENUS

Take this book along to your supermarket or photocopy the list!

Select the same number or size of items that you have in the past, based on the number of people for whom you are shopping. Specific amounts of major ingredients in feature recipes are listed. Review this list before you go to the store. Cross out items that you have on hand and from those meals that you'll be eating away from home. **Write in your breakfast and lunch needs** for the week, as well as you personal likes and needs.

Produce
Potatoes for baking
Broccoli
Melon
Strawberries
Vegetable relishes
Tomatoes
Cucumbers (2 meals)
1 head cabbage
Onions
4 carrots
2 tomatoes
3 scallions
2 red peppers
1/4 cup red onion
1 apple
Celery
Green pepper
Parsley
Banana
4 large sweet potatoes

Bottled/Canned
Red cherries
Orange and grapefruit
   sections in juice
10 oz. can reduced
   sodium tomato soup
4 oz. green chilis
4 cups chicken broth
14 oz. chunky tomatoes

Crushed pineapple in
   juice
Maraschino cherries
15 oz. kidney beans
2 (4 oz. jars) baby food
   carrots
Reduced calorie Italian
   dressing
20 oz. cherry pie filling

Packaged
Soda crackers
2/3 cup quick rice
Walnuts
18 oz. package 94% fat-
   free chocolate cake
   mix
Coconut

Staples/Spices
Salt
Pepper
Vinegar
Dill Weed
Sugar or substitute
Honey
Brown sugar
Dijon mustard
Paprika
Fresh garlic or garlic
   powder
Pepper

White pepper
Lime juice
Vegetable oil
Curry powder
Flour
Lemon juice
Whole cloves
Baking soda
Baking powder
Dried jalapeno
   pepper (optional)
Rum extract
Cardamom
Flour
Cumin
Chili powder
Chicken bouillon
Powdered sugar

Meat Case
4 pork chops
1/2 lb. lean ground
   beef
3 lb. chicken to be
   cooked for soup
2 lb. boneless pork
   roast

Refrigerator Case
Skim milk
Low-fat margarine
Buttermilk
Eggs or liquid substitute

Frozen Case
1 lb. tuna steaks
16 oz. frozen corn

Other
Light beer

Bakery/Deli
Wheat rolls
Rye bread

Non-Food Items
Detergents/Cleaning
Supplies

Paper/Health/
Beauty

Week 4 Dinner Menus At-A-Glance.
Write in Your Own Breakfast and Lunch Ideas.

Breakfast	Lunch	Dinner	Snacks	Do Ahead
Monday		FAST FOOD PICKUP Check out suggestions from your favorite drive-through or CLEAN OUT THE REFRIGERATOR.	Add your choices from Grab a Low-Fat Snack List	Thaw ground beef or turkey for meatloaf.
Tuesday		*Veggie Meatloaf *Picnic Green Beans Baking Powder Biscuit (from a tube) Fresh Nectarine Skim Milk	Choices from Grab a Low-Fat Snack List	Start clam chowder and pound cake for Wednesday.
Wednesday		*New England Clam Chowder French Bread *Pound Cake with Apple Topping Skim Milk	Choices from Grab a Low-Fat Snack List	Thaw meat for burrito.
Thursday		*Baked Burrito *Shredded Zucchini and Yellow Squash Lettuce and Tomato Wedges Fresh Banana Skim Milk	Choices from Grab a Low-Fat Snack List	Boil potatoes for Friday salad.
Friday		*Mom's Night Off Sub Sandwich *Guilt-Free Potato Salad Dill Pickle Spears Nonfat Frozen Yogurt Skim Milk	Choices from Grab a Low-Fat Snack List	Prepare cheesecake for Saturday.
Saturday		*Hot Tamale Supper Lettuce and Tomato Wedges *Strawberry-Filled Cheesecake Light Beer	Choices from Grab a Low-Fat Snack List	Assemble stew. Bake bread for Sunday.
Sunday		*Rio Grande Stew *Carrot Orange Zucchini Bread *Blueberry Crumble Skim Milk	Choices from Grab a Low-Fat Snack List	Assemble and re-frigerate casse-role, thaw beef, prepare pudding for Monday.

*See Day-at-a-Glance Menus for Serving Sizes

SHOPPING LIST FOR WEEK 4 DINNER MENUS

Take this book along to your supermarket or photocopy the list!
Select the same number or size of items that you have in the past, based on the number of people for whom you are shopping. Specific amounts of major ingredients in feature recipes are listed. Review this list before you go to the store. Cross out items that you have on hand and from those meals that you'll be eating away from home. **Write in your breakfast and lunch needs** for the week, as well as your personal likes and needs.

Produce
Nectarines
Lettuce
Tomato
Bananas
1 lb. carrots
Celery
Parsley
2 lb. green beans or 2
   (1 lb.) cans green
   beans
Onions
3 large red-skinned
   potatoes
5 baking potatoes
2 cooking apples
Scallions
5 zucchini
3 yellow squash
1 tomato
3 cups blueberries
1 cup strawberries
2 cups fresh cabbage

Bottled/Canned
Dill pickles
16 oz. no-added-salt
   tomato sauce
8 oz. mushrooms
1 cup reduced sodium
   tomato soup
8 oz. clam broth
1 cup evaporated skim
   milk
16 1/2 oz. minced
   clams
Reduced fat or non-
   fat mayonnaise
2 (15 oz.) cans beef
   broth

15 oz. tomato paste
1 1/2 cups corn
4 oz. green chilis
4 oz. baby food carrots

Packaged
18 oz. package 94%
   fat-free yellow
   cake mix
Raisins
Almonds
16 graham cracker
   squares
3 1/2 oz. package
   lemon gelatin
Oatmeal
Parmesan cheese

Staples/Spices
Fresh garlic or garlic
   powder
Nutmeg
Worcestershire
   sauce
Dry mustard
Oregano
Brown sugar
Prepared mustard
Flour
Thyme
Hot pepper sauce
Cinnamon
Almond extract
Cumin
Cayenne (optional)
Dried jalapeno
   pepper (optional)
Sugar or substitute
Lemon juice
Chives
Bay leaf

Honey
Vinegar
Cornmeal
Vegetable oil
Oregano
Chili powder
Coriander
Cornstarch
Orange and vanilla
   extract
Baking powder
Wheat flour
Salt and pepper

Meat Case
3 1/2 lb. lean ground
   beef
1 lb. stew meat

Refrigerator Case
Skim milk
Low-fat margarine
Baking powder
   biscuit dough
Eggs or liquid
   substitute
8 flour tortillas
4 oz. part-skim American
   cheese
4 oz. reduced fat
   Swiss cheese
2 cups low-fat cottage
   cheese

Frozen Case
Nonfat frozen yogurt
10 oz. corn
Orange juice
   concentrate
2 cups light whipped
   topping

Other
Light beer

Bakery/Deli
French bread (2 meals)
1/2 lb. lean ham (to
   save money,
   purchase ham from
   meat case, and ask
   deli department to
   slice it)
1/4 lb. turkey
Your choice of bread
   for toast

Non-Food Items
Detergents/
Cleaning Supplies

Paper/Health/
Beauty

Week 5 Dinner Menus At-A-Glance.
Write in Your Own Breakfast and Lunch Ideas.

Breakfast	Lunch	Dinner	Snacks	Do Ahead
Monday		Broiled Lean Ground Beef Patty on Toast *Broccoli Rice Casserole Fresh Green Salad with No-Oil Dressing *Pumpkin Pudding Skim Milk	Choices from Grab a Low-Fat Snack List	Thaw chicken and start carrot salad for Tuesday.
Tuesday		*No-Fat Fried Chicken *Carrot Marinade Baked Potato Wheat Toast Low-Fat Margarine Grapefruit and Orange Sections Skim Milk	Choices from Grab a Low-Fat Snack List	Relax!
Wednesday		FAST FOOD PICKUP Check out suggestions from your favorite drive-through or CLEAN OUT THE REFRIGERATOR.	Add your choices from Grab a Low-Fat Snack List	Thaw bread for Thursday.
Thursday		*Egg and Cheese Braid Fresh Vegetable Relishes Tomato Juice Sherbet with Pineapple on Top Skim Milk	Choices from Grab a Low-Fat Snack List	Thaw chicken and start pudding for Friday.
Friday		*California Blend Vegetables with Chicken Fresh Cucumber and Tomato Wedges with Low-Fat Buttermilk or Italian Dressing *Peach Pudding Skim Milk	Choices from Grab a Low-Fat Snack List	Thaw halibut and make brownies for Saturday.
Saturday		*Pumpkin Soup with Croutons *Grilled Halibut with Pineapple Salsa *Vegetable Stuffing *Zucchini Brownies Skim Milk	Choices from Grab a Low-Fat Snack List	Thaw sirloin and start trifle for Sunday.
Sunday		*Beer Grilled Sirloin *Good Fortune Chinese Vegetables Hard Roll Low-Fat Margarine *English Trifle Skim Milk	Choices from Grab a Low-Fat Snack List	Thaw ground beef for Monday.

*See Day-at-a-Glance Menus for Serving Sizes

Shopping List for Week 5 Dinner Menus

Take this book along to your supermarket or photocopy the list!
Select the same number or size of items that you have in the past, based on the
number of people for whom you are shopping. Specific amounts of major
ingredients in feature recipes are listed. Review this list before you go to the
store. Cross out items that you have on hand and from those meals that you'll
be eating away from home. **Write in your breakfast and lunch needs** for
the week, as well as your personal likes and needs.

Produce
Grapes
Potatoes for baking
Vegetables for relish
Cucumbers
Tomatoes
1 cup celery
1/2 cup onion
8 oz. mushrooms
4 peaches or nectarines
or 16 oz. canned
peaches in juice
1 cup berries of choice
1 lb. carrots
1 large green pepper
Scallions
Pineapple
1 red pepper
5 cups zucchini
2 cups veggies of choice
for stirfry
2 cups berries or fresh
fruit

Bottled/Canned
No-oil dressing
Grapefruit and orange
sections in juice
Tomato juice
Cran-raspberry juice
Low-fat buttermilk
dressing
1/3 cup Parmesan
cheese
1/2 cup bread crumbs
8 oz. tomato sauce
10 oz. Campbell's
Healthy Request
Cream of Chicken
Soup

2 (16 oz.) cans pumpkin
4 cups no-added-salt
chicken broth
1 cup evaporated skim
milk
1/4 cup reduced sodium
soy sauce
Oyster sauce

Packaged
Quick rice
3 1/2 oz. sugar-free
or regular lemon
gelatin
Croutons
1 package herbed
stuffing mix
1/3 cup coconut
1/2 cup sliced
almonds
8 oz. package 94%
fat-free yellow cake
mix
3 1/2 oz. instant
vanilla pudding mix

Staples/Spices
Salt
Pepper
Nonfat dry milk
Cornstarch
Chicken bouillon
Dried onion
Basil
Thyme
Rosemary
Fresh garlic or garlic
powder
Onion powder
Vinegar
Brown sugar

Prepared mustard
Celery seed
Lemon juice
Poppy seeds
Vanilla
Cinnamon
Nutmeg
Ginger
Dijon mustard
Dried cilantro
Lime juice
Vegetable oil
Flour
Soda
Cocoa

Meat Case
4 chicken breast
halves
1 lb. boneless chicken
1 lb. sirloin

Refrigerator Case
Skim milk
Low-fat margarine
Reduced fat
American cheese
3/4 cup buttermilk
10 eggs or liquid
substitute
4 oz. reduced fat
Swiss cheese
1 tube pizza crust
1/2 cup tofu

Frozen Case
Sherbet
3 (10 oz.) packages
broccoli pieces

16 oz. California
blend vegetables
1 lb. halibut or firm
white fish

Other
1 cup beer
Dry sherry

Bakery/Deli
Hard rolls
4 oz. lean ham

Non-Food Items
Detergents/
Cleaning Supplies

Paper/Health/
Beauty

59

WEEK 6 DINNER MENUS AT-A-GLANCE.
WRITE IN YOUR OWN BREAKFAST AND LUNCH IDEAS.

Breakfast	Lunch	Dinner	Snacks	Do Ahead
Monday		*Microwave Meat-loaf *Orange Glazed Sugar Snap Peas Leftover Hard Rolls Chunky Applesauce Skim Milk	Choices from Grab a Low-Fat Snack List	Start beans for Tuesday.
Tuesday		GO MEATLESS *Sandy's Red Beans and Rice Toasted Bagel with Low-Fat Cheese Sliced Kiwifruit Skim Milk	Choices from Grab a Low-Fat Snack List	Thaw meat for pizza topping for Wednesday.
Wednesday		*Pour Pizza-Lettuce Salad with No-Oil Dressing *Coffee-Flavored Chocolate Brownies Skim Milk	Choices from Grab a Low-Fat Snack List	Get potatoes and ham ready for the crockpot and start first thing Thursday morning.
Thursday		*Crockpot Potatoes with Ham *Maple Syrup Muffins Carrot Sticks Cran-Raspberry Juice Skim Milk	Choices from Grab a Low-Fat Snack List	Relax!
Friday		FAST FOOD PICKUP Check out suggestions from your favorite drive-through or CLEAN OUT THE REFRIGERATOR.	Add your choices from Grab a Low-Fat Snack List	Thaw steak for Saturday.
Saturday		*Steak Picado Raw Cauliflower *Raisin Bread in the Microwave Low-Fat Margarine *Rhubarb Dream Dessert Skim Milk	Choices from Grab a Low-Fat Snack List	Thaw chicken and make shell for pavlova for Sunday.
Sunday		*Hula Chicken with Rice Green Salad with No-Oil Dressing *Pavlova Skim Milk	Choices from Grab a Low-Fat Snack List	Relax!

*See Day-at-a-Glance Menus for Serving Sizes

Shopping List for Week 6 Dinner Menus

Take this book along to your supermarket or photocopy the list!
Select the same number or size of items that you have in the past, based on the
number of people for whom you are shopping. Specific amounts of major
ingredients in feature recipes are listed. Review this list before you go to the
store. Cross out items that you have on hand and from those meals that you'll
be eating away from home. **Write in your breakfast and lunch needs** for
the week, as well as your personal likes and needs.

Produce
Kiwifruit
Lettuce
Carrots
Cauliflower
Salad greens
4 medium onions
Fresh vegetable
  toppings for pizza
3 large green peppers
1 large tomato
4 cups rhubarb or
  cooking apples such
  as Jonathan or
  Macintosh
1 lime

Bottled/Canned
Chunky applesauce
No-oil dressing
Cran-raspberry juice
No-added-salt tomato
  sauce
1 1/2 cups pizza sauce
  of choice
Instant coffee
10 oz. Campbell's
  Healthy Request
  Cream of Chicken
  Soup
Maple syrup
10 oz. pineapple slices

Packaged
Oatmeal
2 lb. red beans (dry)
Quick rice
Dry yeast
1/3 cup instant potatoes
1/4 cup Parmesan
  cheese
18 oz. package 94%
  fat-free brownie mix
3/4 cup bran cereal
2 TB. walnuts
1/2 cup raisins
3 1/2 oz. sugar-free
  or regular
  strawberry
  gelatin

Staples/Spices
Salt
Pepper
Brown sugar
Prepared mustard
Thyme
Fresh garlic or garlic
  powder
Worcestershire
  sauce
Hot pepper sauce
Vegetable oil
Flour
Powdered sugar

Baking powder
Cumin
2 cups self-rising
  flour
Sugar
Cinnamon
Nutmeg
Honey
Soy sauce
Cornstarch
Vinegar

Meat Case
1 lb. lean ground beef
1 lb. sirloin
2 whole skinned
  chicken breasts,
  split

Refrigerator Case
Skim milk
Low-fat margarine
Choice of reduced fat
  cheese for slicing
Eggs or liquid
  substitute
2 slices bacon
4 oz. part-skim
  mozzarella cheese
1 cup buttermilk

1/2 cup reduced fat
  cheddar cheese
  spread

Frozen Case
1 lb. sugar snap peas
Orange juice
  concentrate
1 lb. frozen
  hashbrowns

Other
3 cups red wine
12 oz. beer

Bakery/Deli
Bagels
8 oz. lean ham

Non-Food Items
Detergents/
Cleaning Supplies

Paper/Health/
Beauty

Week 7 Dinner Menus At-A-Glance.
Write in Your Own Breakfast and Lunch Ideas.

Breakfast	Lunch	Dinner	Snacks	Do Ahead
Monday		FAST FOOD PICKUP Check out suggestions from your favorite drive-through or CLEAN OUT THE REFRIGERATOR.	Add your choices from Grab a Low-Fat Snack List	Thaw meat for fajita on Tuesday.
Tuesday		*Fajita Pita Chopped Lettuce and Tomatoes Peach Sauce with Fresh Bananas Skim Milk	Choices from Grab a Low-Fat Snack List	Thaw ground beef for Wednesday.
Wednesday		Broiled Hamburger Patty on a Bun *Five Bean Sweet and Sour Salad Fresh Pear Skim Milk	Choices from Grab a Low-Fat Snack List	Thaw ground turkey, pork or beef for meat loaf on Thursday.
Thursday		*Microwave Meatloaf Baked Potato with Low-Fat Margarine Steamed Peas and Carrots Strawberries on Vanilla Ice Milk or Nonfat Frozen Dessert Skim Milk	Choices from Grab a Low-Fat Snack List	Relax!
Friday		*Taco Rice Delight Chopped Lettuce and Tomatoes Chunky Fruits in Sugar-Free Ginger Ale Skim Milk	Choices from Grab a Low-Fat Snack List	Thaw fish for Saturday. Start gazpacho and bread pudding for Saturday.
Saturday		*My Favorite Gazpacho *Tasty Marinated Grilled White Fish Steamed Brown Rice *Miss Pat's Bread Pudding Skim Milk	Choices from Grab a Low-Fat Snack List	Thaw roast and bake cake for Sunday.
Sunday		*Crockpot Beef Roast with Fat-Free Gravy Boiled Red Skinned Potatoes Steamed Fresh Broccoli *You'll Love Chutney *Better Than Sex Cake Skim Milk	Choices from Grab a Low-Fat Snack List	Thaw chicken for Monday.

*See Day-at-a-Glance Menus for Serving Sizes

SHOPPING LIST FOR WEEK 7 DINNER MENUS

Take this book along to your supermarket or photocopy the list!
Select the same number or size of items that you have in the past, based on the number of people for whom you are shopping. Specific amounts of major ingredients in feature recipes are listed. Review this list before you go to the store. Cross out items that you have on hand and from those meals that you'll be eating away from home. **Write in your breakfast and lunch needs** for the week, as well as your personal likes and needs.

Produce
Lettuce (2 meals)
Tomatoes (2 meals)
Banana
Pears
Potatoes for baking
Strawberries
Red-skinned potatoes
Broccoli
1 pepper
1 large onion
1 large cucumber
Scallions
Fresh lemon for juice

Bottled/Canned
Peaches in juice
Chunky fruits in juice
16 oz. green beans
16 oz. lima beans
16 oz. wax beans
16 oz. kidney beans
16 oz. garbanzo beans
16 oz. no-added-salt
    tomato sauce
1/2 cup salsa
Quick rice
1 cup no-added-salt
    tomato juice
1 cup pineapple tidbits
    in juice
10 oz. crushed
    pineapple in juice

Packaged
Regular or sugar-free
    gelatin, choose your
    favorite flavor
Oatmeal
Brown rice
1 1/4 cup coconut
3/4 cup raisins
Dry vegetable soup
    mix
1/3 cup dried apricot
18 oz. package 94%
    fat-free yellow cake
    mix
2 (3 1/2 oz.) packages
    vanilla instant
    pudding

Staples/Spices
Salt
Pepper
Vegetable oil
Lime juice
Sugar
Cornstarch
Vinegar
Brown sugar
Prepared mustard
Thyme
2 tsp. dried jalapeno
    pepper
Red wine vinegar
Fresh garlic or garlic
    powder

Sugar
Parsley
2 TB. ketchup
Cornstarch
Sugar
Cinnamon
Nutmeg
Powdered sugar
Rum extract
Cider vinegar
Ginger
Cumin

Meat Case
Lean ground beef
    (3 meals)
1 lb. boneless
    chicken, in strips
2 lb. chuck roast

Refrigerator Case
Skim milk
Low-fat margarine
8 slices bacon
Eggs or liquid
    substitute
2 oz. part-skim
    cheddar cheese

Frozen Case
Peas and carrots
Vanilla ice milk
4 pita pockets
Orange juice

Other
12 oz. beer

Bakery/Deli
Hamburger buns
6 cups bread cubes
    for bread pudding

Non-Food Items
Detergents/
Cleaning Supplies

Paper/Health/
Beauty

WEEK 8 DINNER MENUS AT-A-GLANCE.
WRITE IN YOUR OWN BREAKFAST AND LUNCH IDEAS.

Breakfast	Lunch	Dinner	Snacks	Do Ahead
Monday		*Chicken and Noodles in Red Sauce *Tangy Green Beans Fresh Carrot Sticks Blueberries in Sauce Skim Milk	Choices from Grab a Low-Fat Snack List	Relax!
Tuesday		Low-Fat Hot Dog on a Bun *Brussels Sprouts Polanaise Dill Pickle Spears Chocolate Ice Milk Cran-Raspberry Juice	Choices from Grab a Low-Fat Snack List	Relax!
Wednesday		FAST FOOD PICKUP Check out suggestions from your favorite drive-through or CLEAN OUT THE REFRIGERATOR.	Add your choices from Grab a Low-Fat Snack List	Thaw chicken and make pudding for Thursday.
Thursday		*Cornflake Chicken *BBQ Baked Potatoes Steamed Sugar Snap Peas Butterscotch Pudding made with Skim Milk	Choices from Grab a Low-Fat Snack List	May put together lasagne for Friday.
Friday		*Time Saver Lasagne Fresh Green Salad with No-Oil Dressing French Bread Low-Fat Margarine Melon Wedges Skim Milk	Choices from Grab a Low-Fat Snack List	May start chili and make bread for Saturday.
Saturday		*Cocktail Crab Dip with Vegetable Dippers and Bread-sticks *Best of Show Chili *Tangy Carrot and Raisin Salad *Poppy Seed Bread Skim Milk	Choices from Grab a Low-Fat Snack List	May thaw fish and make cake for Sunday.
Sunday		*Crusty Fish with Herbs Baked Potato Low-Fat Margarine *San Francisco Coleslaw *Raspberry Filled Chocolate Cake Skim Milk	Choices from Grab a Low-Fat Snack List	Relax!

*See Day-at-a-Glance Menus for Serving Sizes

SHOPPING LIST FOR WEEK 8 DINNER MENUS

Take this book along to your supermarket or photocopy the list!
Select the same number or size of items that you have in the past, based on the number of people for whom you are shopping. Specific amounts of major ingredients in feature recipes are listed. Review this list before you go to the store. Cross out items that you have on hand and from those meals that you'll be eating away from home. **Write in your breakfast and lunch needs** for the week, as well as your personal likes and needs.

Produce
Carrots
Greens for salad
Melon
Vegetables for dipping
Potatoes
3 onions
2 lb. green beans
1 lb. Brussels sprouts
Parsley
1 lemon for juice
2 peppers
Apples
1 orange
1 lb. shredded cabbage
1 red onion

Bottled/Canned
Dill pickles
Cran-raspberry juice
No-oil dressing
3 (14 oz.) cans chunky
    tomatoes
1 1/2 cups evaporated
    skim milk
16 oz. tomato sauce
2 (16 oz.) cans kidney
    beans
2/3 cups reduced sugar
    raspberry jam

Packaged
Sugar-free or regular
    butterscotch pudding
Breadsticks
Choice of noodles
3 cups crushed
    cornflakes
9 lasagne noodles
1/2 cup almonds
1/2 oz. unsweetened
    chocolate
2/3 cup raisins
1/2 cup bread crumbs
18 oz. 94% fat-free
    chocolate cake mix

Staples/Spices
Salt
Pepper
Fresh garlic or garlic
    powder
Rosemary
Basil
Vegetable oil
Cider vinegar
Brown sugar
Sugar
Dijon mustard
Lemon juice
Flour
Ketchup
Worcestershire
    sauce
Thyme

Horseradish
Lemon juice
Celery seeds
Prepared mustard
Oregano
MSG or Accent
Paprika
Chili powder
Cumin
Dry mustard
Baking powder
Vanilla
Poppy seeds
Almond extract
Powdered sugar

Meat Case
4 chicken breasts
1 lb. chicken skinned
    in pieces
1 lb. lean ground beef

Refrigerator Case
Skim milk
Low-fat margarine
Reduced fat hot dogs
Eggs or liquid
    substitute
2 slices bacon
2 oz. reduced fat
    American cheese
1 1/2 cup part-skim
    ricotta cheese

4 oz. part-skim
    mozzarella cheese
1 oz. part-skim
    cheddar cheese
4 oz. light cream
    cheese
4 oz. mock crab

Frozen Case
Blueberries
Chocolate ice milk
Sugar snap peas
1/2 cup orange juice
    concentrate
1 lb. frozen white fish
    fillets

Other
1/4 cup dry white
    wine

Bakery/Deli
Hot dog buns

Non-Food Items
Detergents/
Cleaning Supplies

Paper/Health/
Beauty

Week 9 Dinner Menus At-A-Glance.
Write in Your Own Breakfast and Lunch Ideas.

Breakfast	Lunch	Dinner	Snacks	Do Ahead
Monday		GO MEATLESS. *Kids Love This 　Cheese Soup *Hurry Up Sweet 　and Sour Salad Broiled French Bread Fresh Banana Skim Milk	Choices from Grab a Low-Fat Snack List	Put casserole to- gether in the crockpot for Tuesday.
Tuesday		*Kraut Casserole in 　the Crockpot Rye Bread Low-Fat Margarine Apple Slices Skim Milk	Choices from Grab a Low-Fat Snack List	Thaw fish for Wednesday.
Wednesday		*White Fish with 　Vegetables in the 　Microwave Fresh Cherry Tomatoes White Dinner Roll Low-Fat Margarine Tropical Fruit Blend Skim Milk	Choices from Grab a Low-Fat Snack List	Thaw ground meat for Thursday.
Thursday		*Mexican Corn Main- 　dish Corn Bread Muffin 　from a Mix Low-Fat Margarine Green Grapes Skim Milk	Choices from Grab a Low-Fat Snack List	Start soup for Friday.
Friday		*Turkey Vegetable 　Soup *Salmon Spread for 　Crackers Low-Fat Wheat Crackers Sherbet Skim Milk	Choices from Grab a Low-Fat Snack List	May prepare cake for Saturday.
Saturday		*Shrimp Creole Fresh Green Salad 　with *Make Your 　Own Buttermilk 　Dressing *Shortcake for 　Strawberries Skim Milk	Choices from Grab a Low-Fat Snack List	Thaw chicken for Sunday. Bake cake for Sunday.
Sunday		*Italian Chicken 　with Cheese *Fabulous French 　Bread *Zucchini with 　Almonds *Lemon Angel Cake 　with Walnuts Skim Milk	Choices from Grab a Low-Fat Snack List	Make a plan for Monday.

*See Day-at-a-Glance Menus for Serving Sizes

SHOPPING LIST FOR WEEK 9 DINNER MENUS

Take this book along to your supermarket or photocopy the list!
Select the same number or size of items that you have in the past, based on the
number of people for whom you are shopping. Specific amounts of major
ingredients in feature recipes are listed. Review this list before you go to the
store. Cross out items that you have on hand and from those meals that you'll
be eating away from home. **Write in your breakfast and lunch needs** for
the week, as well as your personal likes and needs.

Produce
Bananas
Apples
Cherry tomatoes
Grapes
Fresh greens for salad
Strawberries
1 bunch celery
1 lb. carrots
3 large onions
5 potatoes
Parsley
6 zucchini
8 oz. mushrooms
1 orange
1 lemon
1/2 lb. green beans
1 pepper

Bottled/Canned
Tropical fruit blend
 in juice
3 1/2 cups chicken
 broth
32 oz. sauerkraut
7 oz. green chiles
2 (14 oz.) cans chunky
 tomatoes
15 oz. salmon
6 oz. tomato paste
1 cup reduced or nonfat
 mayonnaise

Packaged
Corn bread mix
Low-fat wheat crackers
Cornmeal
3 cups quick rice

1/4 cup Parmesan
 cheese
2 TB. sliced almonds
18 oz. angel food
 cake mix

Staples/Spices
Salt
Pepper
Flour
Paprika
Sugar
Vinegar
Prepared mustard
Brown sugar
Thyme
Fresh garlic or
 garlic powder
Lemon juice
Worchestershire sauce
Ketchup
Horseradish
Dill weed
Liquid smoke
 (optional)
Basil
Cayenne pepper
Soy sauce
Bay leaf
MSG
Dried parsley
White pepper
Onion powder
Sugar
Oregano
Dry yeast
Marjoram

Meat Case
1 lb. ground beef
1 cup cooked turkey
2 chicken breasts,
 skinned and split

Refrigerator Case
Skim milk
Low-fat margarine
4 oz. reduced fat
 cheddar cheese
6 slices bacon
1/2 cup nonfat yogurt
1 cup shredded part-
 skim mozzarella
 cheese
4 oz. light cream
 cheese
1 cup buttermilk
2 (10 oz.) tubes
 buttermilk biscuits
2 oz. reduced fat
 American cheese
Eggs or liquid substitute

Frozen Case
Sherbet
20 oz. mixed
 vegetables
1 lb. white fish fillets,
 not more than 1/2
 inch thick
10 oz. corn
1 lb. shrimp
1/2 cup lemonade
 concentrate

Other
1/2 cup dry white wine
Cream sherry

Bakery/Deli
French bread
Rye bread
Dinner rolls
1/2 lb. lean ham

Non-Food Items
Detergents/
Cleaning Supplies

Paper/Health/
Beauty

* * * * *

Daily Menus

WEEK 1 MONDAY MENUS

Menu	Serving Sizes		
	1200 cal. 33 gms. fat	1500 cal. 42 gms. fat	1800 cal. 50 gms. fat
Breakfast			
Choice of Fruit Juice	1/2 c.	1/2 c.	1/2 c.
*Breakfast in the Car	1	1	1
Skim Milk	1 c.	1 c.	1 c.
Coffee or Tea	As Desired	As Desired	As Desired
Lunch			
Sliced Lean Ham	2 oz.	3 oz.	3 oz.
French Bread	2 slices	3 slices	3 slices
Mustard	As Desired	As Desired	As Desired
Light Potato Chips	4	9	9
Fresh Veggies	1 c.	1 c.	1 c.
Green Grapes	12	12	24
Iced Tea	As Desired	As Desired	As Desired
Dinner			
*Fajitas with Iowa Beef	1 serving	1 serving	1 serving
Flour Tortilla on the side	none	1	2
Lettuce and Tomatoes	As Desired	As Desired	As Desired
*Pina Colada Fruit Salad	1/2 c.	1/2 c.	1 c.
Skim Milk	1 c.	1 c.	1 c.
Grab a Snack choices	85 cal. 5 gm. fat	110 cal. 5 gm. fat	110 cal. 5 gm. fat

Do Ahead:
Start salad for Tuesday lunch.
Start soup for Tuesday dinner.

WEEK 1 TUESDAY MENUS

Menu	Serving Sizes		
	1200 cal. 33 gms. fat	1500 cal. 42 gms. fat	1800 cal. 50 gms. fat
Breakfast			
Grape Juice	1/3 c.	1/3 c.	1/3 c.
Hot Cereal	1/2 c.	1/2 c.	1/2 c.
Toasted Bagel	1	1	1
Low-fat Margarine	1 tsp.	2 tsp.	2 tsp.
Skim Milk	1 c.	1 c.	1 c.
Coffee or Tea	As Desired	As Desired	As Desired
Lunch			
*Greek Tuna and Pasta Salad	1 c.	1 c.	1 c.
Bagel	none	1/2	1/2
Raisins	2 TB.	2 TB.	4 TB.
Mineral Water	As Desired	As Desired	As Desired
Dinner			
*Hamburger Soup	2 c.	2 c.	2 c.
Soda Crackers	none	3	6
*Crunchy Broccoli Salad	1 c.	1 c.	1 c.
Tropical Fruit Blend	1/2 c.	1/2 c.	1 c..
Skim Milk	1 c.	1/2 c.	1 c.
Grab A Snack choices	85 cal. 5 gms. fat	125 cal. 5 gms. fat	150 cal. 5 gms. fat

Do Ahead:
Thaw chicken breasts for Wednesday dinner.

* Recipes are included in.this book. Check index for page numbers.

WEEK 1 WEDNESDAY MENUS

Menu	Serving Sizes		
	1200 cal. 33 gms. fat	1500 cal. 42 gms. fat	1800 cal. 50 gms. fat
Breakfast			
Choice of Juice	1/2 c.	1/2 c.	1/2 c.
Bran Cereal	1/2 c.	1/2 c.	1/2 c.
Fresh Berries	1 c.	1 c.	1 c.
Wheat Toast	1	1	1
Low-fat Margarine	1 tsp.	2 tsp.	2 tsp.
Skim Milk	1 c.	1 c.	1 c.
Coffee or Tea	As Desired	As Desired	As Desired
Lunch			
Leftover Hamburger Soup	1 c.	2 c.	2 c.
Soda Crackers	none	3	3
Fresh Orange	1	1	2
Diet Soft Drink	As Desired	As Desired	As Desired
Dinner			
Grilled Chicken Breast	4 oz.	4 oz.	4 oz.
Hamburger Roll	1/2	1/2	1
Lettuce and Tomato	As Desired	As Desired	As Desired
Corn on the Cob	1/2	1	1
Low-fat Margarine	1 tsp.	2 tsp.	4 tsp.
Fresh Pineapple	1/2 c.	1/2 c.	1 c.
Skim Milk	1 c.	1 c.	1 c.
Grab A Snack choices	60 cal. 0 gms. fat	125 cal. 5 gms. fat	150 cal. 5 gms. fat

Do Ahead:
Make muffins for breakfast.

WEEK 1 THURSDAY MENUS

Menu	Serving Sizes		
	1200 cal. 33 gms. fat	1500 cal. 42 gms. fat	1800 cal. 50 gms. fat
Breakfast			
Orange Juice	1/2 c.	1/2 c.	1/2 c.
*Banana Breakfast Muffin	1	1	1
Oatmeal with Raisins	1/2 c.	1/2 c.	1/2 c.
Skim Milk	1 c.	1 c.	1 c.
Coffee or Tea	As Desired	As Desired	As Desired
Lunch			
Leftover Chicken Breast	2 oz.	3 oz.	3 oz.
Wheat Bread	1 slice	2 slices	2 slices
Lettuce, Pickles, Mustard	As Desired	As Desired	As Desired
Light Potato Chips	4	9	9
Fresh Apple	1	1	2
Hot Tea	As Desired	As Desired	As Desired
Dinner			
*Spanish Pork Chops with Peppers	2 oz. meat 1 c. veg.	3 oz. meat 1 c. veg.	3 oz. meat 1 c. veg.
Baked Potato	1/2	1	1
Corn Muffin	1/2	1	2
Low-fat Margarine	none	none	2 tsp.
*Cabbage Salad with Poppy Seed Dressing	1 1/2 c.	1 1/2 c.	1 1/2 c.
Kiwifruit	1	1	2
Skim Milk	1 c.	1 c.	1 c.
Grab A Snack choices	95 cal. 5 gms. fat	95 cal. 5 gms. fat	120 cal. 5 gms. fat

Do Ahead:
Start salad for Friday lunch.

* Recipes are included in this book. Check index for page numbers.

WEEK 1 FRIDAY MENUS

Menu	Serving Sizes		
	1200 cal. 33 gms. fat	1500 cal. 42 gms. fat	1800 cal. 50 gms. fat
Breakfast			
Low-fat Yogurt	1 c.	1 c.	1 c.
Fresh Fruit	1	1	1
Toast	1	1	1
Low-fat Margarine	1 tsp.	2 tsp.	12 tsp.
or a Leftover Muffin	1	1	1
Skim Milk	1 c.	1 c.	1 c.
Coffee or Tea	As Desired	As Desired	As Desired
Lunch			
*Creole Shrimp Salad	2 c.	2 c.	2 c.
Leftover Corn Muffin	1	1	1
Cranberry Juice	1/2 c.	1/2 c.	1 c.

Dinner
Fast Food Pickup, check index for page number for menu ideas, or Clean Out the Refrigerator.

Grab-a-Snack choices:	95 cal. 8 gms. fat	125 cal. 5 gms. fat	175 cal. 5 gms. fat

Do Ahead:
Start raisin bread, potatoes, cookies and dip for Saturday.

WEEK 1 SATURDAY MENUS

Menu	Serving Sizes		
	1200 cal. 33 gms. fat	1500 cal. 42 gms. fat	1800 cal. 50 gms. fat
Breakfast			
Choice of Juice	1/2 c	1/2 c.	1/2 c.
*Sportsman's Breakfast	1 serving	1 serving	1 serving
*Crunchy Raisin Bread	none	1 slice	1 slice
Skim Milk	1 c.	1 c.	1 c.
Coffee or tea	As Desired	As Desired	As Desired
Lunch			
*Football Saturday Couch Potatoes	1 skin	1 skin	2 skin
*Hot Broccoli Dip with French Bread Dippers	3/4 c.	3/4 c.	3/4 c.
Fresh Veggies	As Desired	As Desired	As Desired
Light Beer	1/2 can	1 can	1 can
Dinner			
*Potato, Green Bean and Bacon Supper Salad	1 1/2 c.	1 1/2 c.	1 1/2 c.
*Beer and Cheese Biscuits	none	1	1
*Snickerdoodles	none	none	1
Skim Milk	1 c.	1 c.	1 c.
Grab-A-Snack choices	45 cal. 0 gms. fat	50 cal. 0 gms. fat	80 cal. 5 gms. fat

Do Ahead:
Prepare breakfast, pie and cake. Start soup for Sunday.

* Recipes are included in this book. Check index for page numbers.

WEEK 1 SUNDAY MENUS

Menu	Serving Sizes		
	1200 cal. 33 gms. fat	1500 cal. 42 gms. fat	1800 cal. 50 gms. fat
Breakfast			
Cranberry Juice	1/2 c.	1/2 c.	1/2 c.
*Overnight Breakfast Pie	1/16	1/8	1/8
*Cranapple Breakfast Cake	none	1 slice	1 slice
Skim Milk	1/2 c.	1 c.	1 c.
Flavored Coffee	As Desired	As Desired	As Desired
Lunch			
*Chicken Gumbo	2 c.	2 c.	2 c.
Hard Rolls	1	2	2
Low-fat Margarine	none	2 tsp.	2 tsp.
*Old Fashioned Cucumber Salad	1 c.	1 c.	1 c.
Sherbet	1/4 c.	1/4 c.	1/2 c.
Iced Tea	As Desired	As Desired	As Desired
Dinner			
*Beef Burgundy in a French Bread Crust	3 oz.	3 oz.	3 oz.
*Sweet and Sour Bean Salad	1/2 c.	1/2 c.	1 c.
*Glazed Pineapple	1 slice	1 slice	1 slice
Skim Milk	1/2 c.	1 c.	1 c.
Grab-A-Snack choices	40 cal. 0 gms. fat	40 cal. 0 gms. fat	110 cal. 5 gms. fat

Do Ahead:
Start chicken salad, bean casserole and strawberry salad for
Monday.

WEEK 2 MONDAY MENUS

Menu	Serving Sizes		
	1200 cal. 33 gms. fat	1500 cal. 42 gms. fat	1800 cal. 50 gms. fat
Breakfast			
Crunchy Flaked Cereal	1 c.	1 c.	1 c.
Fresh Banana	1/2	1/2	1/2
Wheat Toast	1	1	1
Low-fat Margarine	1/2 tsp	1 tsp.	1 tsp.
Jam	1 tsp.	1 tsp.	1 tsp.
Skim Milk	1 c.	1 c.	1 c.
Coffee or tea	As Desired	As Desired	As Desired
Lunch			
*Not Just Another Chicken Salad	1 c.	1 c.	1 c.
Leftover Hard Rolls	1	2	2
Low-fat Margarine	1 tsp.	2 tsp.	2 tsp.
Leftover Pineapple	1/2 c.	1/2 c.	1 c.
Mineral Water	As Desired	As Desired	As Desired
Dinner			
*Bean Casserole Olé	3/4 c.	1 1/2 c.	1 1/2 c.
Light Corn Chips	none	none	9
*Alison's Strawberry Salad	1/2 c.	1/2 c.	1 c.
Skim Milk	1 c.	1 c.	1 c.
Grab-A-Snack choices	125 cal. 5 gms. fat	180 cal. 5 gms. fat	180 cal. 5 gms. fat

Do Ahead:
Thaw fish for Tuesday. Make muffins for Tuesday breakfast.

* Recipes are included in this book. Check index for page numbers.

WEEK 2 TUESDAY MENUS

Menu	Serving Sizes		
	1200 cal. 33 gms. fat	1500 cal. 42 gms. fat	1800 cal. 50 gms. fat
Breakfast			
*Just Peachy Muffin	1	1	1
Cottage Cheese with	1/4 c.	1/4 c.	1/4 c.
Fresh Fruit	1/2 c.	1/2 c.	1/2 c.
Skim Milk	1 c.	1 c.	1 c.
Coffee or Tea	As Desired	As Desired	As Desired
Lunch			
Leftover Bean Casserole	3/4 c.	3/4 c.	3/4 c.
Leftover Light Corn Chips	none	9	9
Red Grapes	12	12	24
Sugar Free Soft Drink	As Desired	As Desired	As Desired
Dinner			
*Stuffed Sole	3 oz.	4 oz.	4 oz.
*Italian Vegetable Medley	1 c.	1 c.	1 c.
Sherbet	1/4 c.	1/2 c.	1/2 c.
Skim Milk	1 c.	1 c.	1 c.
Grab-A-Snack choices	125 cal. 5 gms. fat	125 cal. 5 gms. fat	125 cal. 5 gms. fat

Do Ahead:
Take the night off!

WEEK 2 WEDNESDAY MENUS

	Serving Sizes		
Menu	**1200 cal.**	**1500 cal.**	**1800 cal.**
	33 gms. fat	**42 gms. fat**	**50 gms. fat**

Breakfast

Apple Juice	1/2 c.	1/2 c.	1/2 c.
Oatmeal	1/2 c.	1/2 c.	1/2 c.
Leftover Muffin	1	1	1
or Toasted Bagel	1	1	1
with Low-fat Margarine	1 tsp.	2 tsp.	2 tsp.
Jam	1 tsp.	1 tsp.	1 tsp.
Skim Milk	1 c.	1 c.	1 c.
Coffee or Tea	As Desired	As Desired	As Desired

Lunch

Peanut Butter & Jelly Sandwich	1/2	1	1
Low-fat Fruited Yogurt	1 c.	1 c.	1 c.
Sparkling Fruit Juice	10 oz.	10 oz.	10 oz.

Dinner

Fast Food Pickup, check index for page number for menu ideas, or Clean Out the Refrigerator.

Grab-A-Snack choices	125 cal.	125 cal.	150 cal.
	5 gms. fat	5 gms. fat	5 gms. fat

Do Ahead:
Start scones, turkey salad and soup for Thursday.

* Recipes are included in this book. Check index for page numbers.

WEEK 2 THURSDAY MENUS

Menu	Serving Sizes		
	1200 cal. 33 gms. fat	1500 cal. 42 gms. fat	1800 cal. 50 gms. fat
Breakfast			
Choice of Juice	1/2 c.	1/2 c.	1/2 c.
*Breakfast Scones	1	1	1
Jam	1 tsp.	1 tsp.	1 tsp.
String Cheese	1 oz.	1 oz.	1 oz.
Fresh Fruit	1/2 c.	1/2 c.	1/2 c.
Skim Milk	1 c.	1 c.	1 c.
Coffee or Tea	As Desired	As Desired	As Desired
Lunch			
*Turkey and Vegetable Salad	3/4 c.	3/4 c.	3/4 c.
Low-fat Wheat Crackers	none	2	2
Fresh Pear	1	1	2
Iced Tea	As Desired	As Desired	As Desired
Dinner			
*Beefy Mushroom & Barley Soup	2 c.	2 c.	2 c.
French Bread	none	1/2 slice	1/2 slice
Low-fat Margarine	none	2 tsp.	4 tsp.
Cherry Tomatoes	As Desired	As Desired	As Desired
Skim Milk	1 c.	1 c.	1 c.
Ice Milk	1/4 c.	1/2 c.	1/2 c
Grab-A Snack choices	105 cal. 5 gms. fat	180 cal. 5 gms. fat	205 cal. 5 gms. fat

Do Ahead:
Start fondue for Friday.

WEEK 2 FRIDAY MENUS

Menu	Serving Sizes		
	1200 cal.	1500 cal.	1800 cal.
	33 gms. fat	42 gms. fat	50 gms. fat

Breakfast

Fresh Grapefruit	1/2	1/2	1/2
Scrambled Egg	1/4 c.	1/4 c.	1/4 c.
Toast	1	2	2
Low-fat Margarine	1 tsp.	2 tsp.	2 tsp.
Jam	1 tsp.	1 tsp.	1 tsp.
Skim Milk	1 c.	1 c.	1 c.
Coffee or Tea	As Desired	As Desired	As Desired

Lunch

Leftover Beefy Mushroom and Barley Soup	1 c.	1 c.	1 c.
Soda Crackers	2	8	8
String Cheese	1/2 oz.	1 oz.	1 oz.
Tropical Fruit Juice	1/2 c.	1/2 c.	1/2 c.

Dinner

*Friday Night Fondue with Raw Veggies and Tortilla Dippers	3/4 c.	3/4 c.	3/4 c.
Red and Green Pea Salad	1/2 c.	1/2 c.	1 c.
Wine Cooler	12 oz.	12 oz.	12 oz.

Grab-A-Snack choices	50 cal.	125 cal.	150 cal.
	9 gms. fat	5 gms. fat	5 gms. fat

Do Ahead:
Start raisin bread. Prepare and refrigerate grits casserole for Saturday.

---

* Recipes are included in this book. Check index for page numbers.

WEEK 2 SATURDAY MENUS

Menu	Serving Sizes		
	1200 cal. 33 gms. fat	1500 cal. 42 gms. fat	1800 cal. 50 gms. fat

Breakfast

*Low-fat Pancakes or French Toast	1	2	2
Applesauce with Maple Flavoring on top	1/2 c.	1/2 c.	1/2 c.
Skim Milk	1 c.	1 c.	1 c.
Coffee or Tea	As Desired	As Desired	As Desired

Lunch

*Salmon & Pasta Salad	1 c.	2 c.	2 c.
Hard Roll	none	1	2
Low-fat Margarine	none	2 tsp.	4 tsp.
*Crunchy Raisin Bread	1 slice	2 slices	2 slices
Fresh Orange Slices	5	5	10
Mineral Water	As Desired	As Desired	As Desired

Dinner

*Hot Berry Wine	none	none	6 oz.
*Broiled Ham with Orange Glaze	2 oz.	3 1/2 oz.	3 1/2 oz.
*Discover Grits Casserole	3/4 c.	1 1/2 c.	1 1/2 c.
Green Salad	As Desired	As Desired	As Desired
Low-fat Dressing	1 tsp.	2 tsp.	2 tsp.
*Cereal Pie Crust with Fruited Filling	1/8th	1/8th	1/8th
Skim Milk	1 c.	1 c.	1 c.

Grab-A-Snack choices	125 cal. 5 gms. fat	125 cal. 5 gms. fat	125 cal. 5 gms. fat

Do Ahead:
Start quiche and lemon ring for Sunday.

WEEK 2 SUNDAY MENUS

	Serving Sizes		
Menu	**1200 cal.**	**1500 cal.**	**1800 cal.**
	33 gms. fat	**42 gms. fat**	**50 gms. fat**

Breakfast

Orange-Pineapple Juice	1/2 c.	1/2 c.	1/2 c.
*Quiche without the Crust	1/8	1/8	1/8
*Lemon Breakfast Ring	1 slice	1 slice	1 slice
Skim Milk	1 c.	1 c.	1 c.
Flavored Coffee	As Desired	As Desired	As Desired

Read the Sunday Paper Lunch

Sliced Turkey rolled with toothpicks	1 oz.	2 oz.	2 oz.
Low-fat Wheat Crackers	4	8	8
String Cheese	1	1	1
Green Apple Slices	1/2 c.	1/2 c.	1 c.
Grape Juice	1/2 c	1/2 c.	1/2 c.

Dinner

*Jambalaya	1 1/2 c.	1 1/2 c.	1 1/2 c.
French Bread	none	1/2 slice	1 1/2 slices
Low-fat margarine	none	2 tsp.	4 tsp.
Green Salad	As Desired	As Desired	As Desired
Low-fat Dressing	1 tsp.	2 tsp.	2 tsp.
Sliced Fresh Pineapple	1/2 c.	1/2 c.	1 c.
Skim Milk	1 c.	1 c.	1 c.

Grab-A-Snack choices

	60 cal.	180 cal.	205 cal.
	0 gms. fat	5 gms. fat	5 gms. fat

Do Ahead:
Thaw chops for Monday.

* Recipes are included in this book. Check index for page numbers.

WEEK 3 MONDAY DINNER MENU

Choose breakfast, lunch and snack items similar to examples in
Week 1 and 2.

Menu	Serving Sizes		
	1200 cal. 33 gms. fat	1500 cal. 42 gms. fat	1800 cal. 50 gms. fat
*Honey Mustard Pork			
Chops	2 oz.	3 oz.	3 oz.
Baked Potato	1	1	1
Low-fat Margarine	1 tsp.	2 tsp.	4 tsp.
Steamed Broccoli	2 c.	2 c.	2 c.
Wheat Dinner Roll	none	1	2
Melon Balls	1 c.	1 c.	2 c.
Skim Milk	1 c.	2 c.	2 c.

Do Ahead:
Assemble casserole for Tuesday.

WEEK 3 TUESDAY DINNER MENU

Choose breakfast, lunch and snack items similar to examples in
Week 1 and 2.

Menu	Serving Sizes		
	1200 cal. 33 gms. fat	1500 cal. 42 gms. fat	1800 cal. 50 gms. fat
*End of the Month			
Vegetable Casserole	3/4 c.	3/4 c.	1 1/2 c.
Rye Bread	none	1 slice	1 slice
Low-fat Margarine	1 tsp.	2 tsp.	4 tsp.
Red Cherries	1/2 c.	1/2 c.	1 c.
Skim Milk	1 c.	1 c.	1 c.

WEEK 3 WEDNESDAY DINNER MENU

Choose breakfast, lunch and snack items similar to examples in Week 1 and 2.

Menu	Serving Sizes		
	1200 cal. 33 gms. fat	1500 cal. 42 gms. fat	1800 cal. 50 gms. fat
*Grilled Tuna Steaks with	2 oz.	3 oz.	3 oz.
*Vegetable Relish	1 c.	1 c.	1 c.
Wheat Rolls	1	2	3
Low-fat Margarine	1 tsp.	2 tsp.	4 tsp.
Orange & Grapefruit			
Sections	1/2 c.	1/2 c.	1 c.
Skim Milk	1 c.	1 c.	1 c.

Do Ahead:
Bake bread and start soup for Thursday.

WEEK 3 THURSDAY DINNER MENU

Choose breakfast, lunch and snack items similar to examples in Week 1 and 2.

Menu	Serving Sizes		
	1200 cal. 33 gms. fat	1500 cal. 42 gms. fat	1800 cal. 50 gms. fat
*Mulligatawney Soup	3 c.	4 c.	4 c.
Soda Crackers	3	3	9
*Aloha Loaf	1/2 slice	1 slice	2 slice
Fresh Strawberries	1 c.	1 c.	2 c.
Skim Milk	1 c.	1 c.	1 c.

Do Ahead:
Relax!

* Recipes are included in this book. Check index for page numbers.

WEEK 3 FRIDAY DINNER MENU

Choose breakfast, lunch and snack items similar to examples in Week 1 and 2.

Check out pages for dinner suggestions from your favorite drive-through or clean out the refrigerator.

Do Ahead:
Start chili, may bake bread and cookies for Saturday.

WEEK 3 SATURDAY DINNER MENU

Choose breakfast, lunch and snack items similar to examples in Week 1 and 2.

Menu	Serving Sizes		
	1200 cal.	**1500 cal.**	**1800 cal.**
	33 gms. fat	**42 gms. fat**	**50 gms. fat**
*Chicken Chili			
without Tomatoes	1 1/2 c.	1 1/2 c.	1 1/2 c.
*Dr. Downey's			
Whole Grain Bread	none	1 slice	2 slices
Low-fat Margarine	none	2 tsp.	4 tsp.
Fresh Relishes	1 c.	1 c.	1 c.
*Carrot Cookies	1/2	1	1
Light Beer	1	1	1

Do Ahead:
Thaw roast, start potatoes, may bake cake for Sunday

WEEK 3 SUNDAY DINNER MENU

Choose breakfast, lunch and snack items similar to examples in
Week 1 and 2.

Menu	Serving Sizes		
	1200 cal. 33 gms. fat	1500 cal. 42 gms. fat	1800 cal. 50 gms. fat
*You Can Microwave Pork Roast	2 oz.	3 oz.	3 oz.
*Tipsy Sweet Potatoes	1/2 serv.	1/2 serv.	1/2 serv.
Tomatoes and Cucumbers sprinkled with Vinegar, Sugar or Substitute and Dill Weed	2 c.	2 c.	2 c.
*Chocolate Cherry Cake with	none	1/2 slice	1 slice
Vanilla Ice Milk on Top	none	none	1/4 c.
Skim Milk	1 c.	1 c.	1 c.

Do Ahead:
Relax!

WEEK 4 MONDAY DINNER MENU

Choose breakfast, lunch and snack items similar to examples in
Week 1 and 2.

Check out pages for dinner suggestions from your favorite drive-
through, or clean out the refrigerator.

Do Ahead:
Thaw ground beef or turkey for meatloaf.

---

* Recipes are included in this book. Check index for page numbers.

WEEK 4 TUESDAY DINNER MENU

Choose breakfast, lunch and snack items similar to examples in Week 1 and 2.

Menu	Serving Sizes		
	1200 cal.	1500 cal.	1800 cal.
	33 gms. fat	42 gms. fat	50 gms. fat
*Veggie Meatloaf	2 oz.	3 oz.	3 oz.
*Picnic Green Beans	2 c.	2 c.	2 c.
Baking Powder Biscuit	1	2	3
Low-fat Margarine	none	none	1 tsp.
Fresh Nectarine	1	1	2
Skim Milk	1 c.	1 c.	1 c.

Do Ahead:

WEEK 4 WEDNESDAY DINNER MENU

Choose breakfast, lunch and snack items similar to examples in Week 1 and 2.

Menu	Serving Sizes		
	1200 cal.	1500 cal.	1800 cal.
	33 gms. fat	42 gms. fat	50 gms. fat
*New England Clam Chowder	1 c.	2 c.	2 c.
French Bread	1 slice	1 slice	2 slices
Low-fat Margarine	1 tsp.	2 tsp.	4 tsp.
*Pound Cake with Apple Topping	1/2 serv.	1/2 serv.	1/2 serv.
Skim Milk	1/2 c.	1/2 c.	1 c.

Do Ahead:
Thaw meat for burrito for Thursday.

WEEK 4 THURSDAY DINNER MENU

Choose breakfast, lunch and snack items similar to examples in Week 1 and 2.

Menu	Serving Sizes		
	1200 cal. 33 gms. fat	1500 cal. 42 gms. fat	1800 cal. 50 gms. fat
*Baked Burrito	1	1 1/2	1 1/2
*Shredded Zucchini and Yellow Squash	1 c.	1 c.	2 c.
Lettuce and Tomato Wedges	1 c.	1 c.	1 c.
Fresh Banana	1/2	1/2	1
Skim Milk	1/2 c.	1 c.	1 c.

Do Ahead:
Boil potatoes for Friday salad.

WEEK 4 FRIDAY DINNER MENU

Choose breakfast, lunch and snack items similar to examples in Week 1 and 2.

Menu	Serving Sizes		
	1200 cal. 33 gms. fat	1500 cal. 42 gms. fat	1800 cal. 50 gms. fat
*Mom's Night Off Sub Sandwich	1/2 serv.	2 serv.	2 serv.
*Guilt-Free Potato Salad	1/2 c.	1/2 c.	1 c.
Dill Pickle Spears	2	2	2
Nonfat Frozen Yogurt	1/4 c.	1/4 c.	1/2 c.
Skim Milk	1 c.	1 c.	1 c.

Do Ahead:
Prepare cheesecake for Saturday.

---

* Recipes are included in this book. Check index for page numbers.

WEEK 4 SATURDAY DINNER MENU

Choose breakfast, lunch and snack items similar to examples in Week 1 and 2.

Menu	Serving Sizes		
	1200 cal. 33 gms. fat	1500 cal. 42 gms. fat	1800 cal. 50 gms. fat
*Hot Tamale Supper	1/2 serv.	1 serv.	1 1/2 serv.
Lettuce and Tomato Wedges	2 c.	2 c.	2 c.
*Strawberry-Filled Cheesecake	1/2 slice	1/2 slice	1 slice
Light Beer	1	1	1

Do Ahead:
Assemble stew and bake bread for Sunday.

WEEK 4 SUNDAY DINNER MENU

Choose breakfast, lunch and snack items similar to examples in Week 1 and 2.

Menu	Serving Sizes		
	1200 cal. 33 gms. fat	1500 cal. 42 gms. fat	1800 cal. 50 gms. fat
*Rio Grande Stew	1 c.	2 c.	3 c.
*Carrot Orange Zucchini Bread	1 slice	1 slice	2 slices
*Blueberry Crumble	1/2 c.	1/2 c.	1 c.
Skim Milk	1 c.	1 c.	1 c.

Do Ahead:
Assemble and refrigerate casserole. Prepare peach pudding for Monday.

WEEK 5 MONDAY DINNER MENU

Choose breakfast, lunch and snack items similar to examples in Week 1 and 2.

Menu	Serving Sizes		
	1200 cal. 33 gms. fat	1500 cal. 42 gms. fat	1800 cal. 50 gms. fat
Broiled Lean Ground Beef Patty	2 oz.	3 oz.	3 oz.
on Toast	none	1 slice	2 slices
Low-fat Margarine	none	none	2 tsp.
Broccoli Rice Casserole	1 1/2 c.	1 1/2 c.	1 1/2 c.
Fresh Green Salad	1 c.	2 c.	2 c.
No-Oil Dressing	2 tsp.	2 tsp.	2 tsp.
*Pumpkin Pudding	6 TB.	3/4 c.	3/4 c.
Skim Milk	1 c.	1 c.	1 c.

Do Ahead:
Thaw chicken and start carrot salad for Tuesday.

WEEK 5 TUESDAY DINNER MENU

Choose breakfast, lunch and snack items similar to examples in Week 1 and 2.

Menu	Serving Sizes		
	1200 cal. 33 gms. fat	1500 cal. 42 gms. fat	1800 cal. 50 gms. fat
*No-Fat Fried Chicken	2 oz.	3 oz.	3 oz.
*Carrot Marinade	3/4 c.	3/4 c.	3/4 c.
Baked Potato	none	1	1
Wheat Toast	none	none	1
Low-fat Margarine	1 tsp.	2 tsp.	4 tsp.
Grapefruit and Orange Sections	1/2 c.	1/2 c.	1 c.
Skim Milk	1 c.	1 c.	1 c.

* Recipes are included in this book. Check index for page numbers.

WEEK 5 WEDNESDAY DINNER MENU

Choose breakfast, lunch and snack items similar to examples in Week 1 and 2.

Check out pages for dinner suggestions from your favorite drive-through or clean out the refrigerator.

Do Ahead:
Start chili. May bake bread and cookies for Saturday.

WEEK 5 THURSDAY DINNER MENU

Choose breakfast, lunch and snack items similar to examples in Week 1 and 2.

Menu	Serving Sizes		
	1200 cal. 33 gms. fat	1500 cal. 42 gms. fat	1800 cal. 50 gms. fat
*Egg and Cheese Braid	1 slice	1 slice	1 slice
Fresh Vegetable Relishes	1 c.	1 c.	1 c.
Tomato Juice	1/2 c.	1/2 c.	1/2 c.
Sherbet	none	1/4 c.	1/2 c.
with Pineapple on Top	1/2 c.	1/2 c.	1 c.
Skim Milk	1 c.	1 c.	1 c.

Do Ahead:
Thaw chicken and start pudding for Friday.

WEEK 5 FRIDAY DINNER MENU

Choose breakfast, lunch and snack items similar to examples in Week 1 and 2.

Menu	Serving Sizes		
	1200 cal. 33 gms. fat	1500 cal. 42 gms. fat	1800 cal. 50 gms. fat
*California Blend Vegetables with Chicken	1/2 serv.	1/2 serv.	1 serv.
Fresh Cucumber and Tomato Wedges with Low-fat Buttermilk or Italian Dressing	1 c.	1 c.	1 c.
*Peach Pudding	1/2 c.	1/2 c.	1 c.
Skim Milk	1 c.	1 1/2 c.	1 1/2 c.

Do Ahead:
Thaw halibut and make brownies for Saturday.

WEEK 5 SATURDAY DINNER MENU

Choose breakfast, lunch and snack items similar to examples in Week 1 and 2.

Menu	Serving Sizes		
	1200 cal. 33 gms. fat	1500 cal. 42 gms. fat	1800 cal. 50 gms. fat
*Pumpkin Soup with Croutons	3/4 c.	3/4 c.	1 1/2 c.
*Grilled Halibut	2 oz.	3 oz.	3 oz.
with Pineapple Salsa	1/2 c.	1/2 c.	1 c.
*Vegetable Stuffing	1/2 c.	1 c.	1 c.
*Zucchini Brownies	none	none	1
Skim Milk	1 c.	1 c.	1 c.

Do Ahead:
Thaw sirloin and start trifle for Sunday.

* Recipes are included in this book. Check index for page numbers.

WEEK 5 SUNDAY DINNER MENU

Choose breakfast, lunch and snack items similar to examples in
Week 1 and 2.

Menu	Serving Sizes		
	1200 cal. 33 gms. fat	1500 cal. 42 gms. fat	1800 cal. 50 gms. fat
*Beer Grilled Sirloin	2 oz.	3 oz.	3 oz.
*Good Fortune Chinese			
Vegetables	1 c.	1 c.	1 c.
Hard Roll	1/2	1	1
Low-fat Margarine	none	2 tsp.	4 tsp.
*English Trifle	none	none	1 serv.
Skim Milk	1 c.	1 c.	1 c.

Do Ahead:
Thaw ground beef for Monday.

WEEK 6 MONDAY DINNER MENU

Choose breakfast, lunch and snack items similar to examples in
Week 1 and 2.

Menu	Serving Sizes		
	1200 cal. 33 gms. fat	1500 cal. 42 gms. fat	1800 cal. 50 gms. fat
*Microwave Meatloaf	2 oz.	3 oz.	3 oz.
*Orange Glazed Sugar			
Snap Peas	1 c.	1 c.	1 c.
Leftover Hard Rolls	1	2	3
Chunky Applesauce	1/2 c.	1/2 c.	1 c.
Skim Milk	1 c.	1 c.	1 c.

Do Ahead:
Start beans for Tuesday.

WEEK 6 TUESDAY DINNER MENU

Choose breakfast, lunch and snack items similar to examples in Week 1 and 2.

Menu	Serving Sizes		
	1200 cal. 33 gms. fat	1500 cal. 42 gms. fat	1800 cal. 50 gms. fat
*Sandy's Red Beans and Rice	2 c.	2 c.	2 c.
Toasted Bagel with Low-fat Cheese on top	none	1/2	1 full
	none	none	2 oz.
Sliced Kiwifruit	1/2 c.	1/2 c.	1 c.
Skim Milk	1/2 c.	1 c.	1 c.

Do Ahead:
Thaw meat for pizza topping for Wednesday.

WEEK 6 WEDNESDAY DINNER MENU

Choose breakfast, lunch and snack items similar to examples in Week 1 and 2.

Menu	Serving Sizes		
	1200 cal. 33 gms. fat	1500 cal. 42 gms. fat	1800 cal. 50 gms. fat
*Pour Pizza	1 serv.	1 serv.	2 serv.
Lettuce Salad	2 c.	2 c.	2 c.
with No-Oil Dressing	2 tsp.	2 tsp.	2 tsp.
*Coffee Chocolate Brownies	none	1	1
Skim Milk	1 c.	1 1/2 c.	1 c.

Do Ahead:
Get potatoes and ham ready for the crockpot and start first thing Thursday morning.

* Recipes are included in this book. Check index for page numbers.

WEEK 6 THURSDAY DINNER MENU

Choose breakfast, lunch and snack items similar to examples in Week 1 and 2.

Menu	Serving Sizes		
	1200 cal. 33 gms. fat	**1500 cal.** 42 gms. fat	**1800 cal.** 50 gms. fat
*Crockpot Potatoes with Ham	1 c.	2 c.	3 c.
*Maple Syrup Muffins	1	1	1
Carrot Sticks	2 c.	2 c.	2 c.
Cran-raspberry Juice	1/2 c.	1/2 c.	1 c.
Skim Milk	1 c.	1 c.	1 c.

Do Ahead:
Relax!

WEEK 6 FRIDAY DINNER MENU

Choose breakfast, lunch and snack items similar to examples in Week 1 and 2.

Check out pages for dinner suggestions from your favorite drive-through or clean out the refrigerator.

Do Ahead:
Thaw steak for Saturday.

WEEK 6 SATURDAY DINNER MENU

Choose breakfast, lunch and snack items similar to examples in
Week 1 and 2.

Menu	Serving Sizes		
	1200 cal. 33 gms. fat	1500 cal. 42 gms. fat	1800 cal. 50 gms. fat
*Steak Picado	1 serv.	1 serv.	1 serv.
Raw Cauliflower	1 c.	1 c.	1 c.
*Raisin Bread in the Microwave	1/2 slice	1 slice	2 slices
Low-fat Margarine	none	2 tsp.	4 tsp.
*Rhubarb Dream Dessert	none	1/2 serv.	1 serv.
Skim Milk	1 c.	1 c.	1 c.

Do Ahead:
Thaw chicken and make shell for pavlova for Sunday.

WEEK 6 SUNDAY DINNER MENU

Choose breakfast, lunch and snack items similar to examples in
Week I and 2.

Menu	Serving Sizes		
	1200 cal. 33 gms. fat	1500 cal. 42 gms. fat	1800 cal. 50 gms. fat
*Hula Chicken	1/2 serv.	1 serv.	1 1/2 serv.
with Rice	1/3 c.	2/3 c.	1 c.
Green Salad	2 c.	2 c.	2 c.
with No-Oil Dressing	2 tsp.	2 tsp.	2 tsp.
*Pavlova	1 serv.	1 serv.	1 serv.
Skim Milk	1 c.	1 c.	1 c.

Do Ahead:
Relax!

* Recipes are included in this book. Check index for page numbers.

WEEK 7 MONDAY DINNER MENU

Choose breakfast, lunch and snack items similar to examples in Week 1 and 2.

Check out pages for dinner suggestions from your favorite drive-through or clean out the refrigerator.

Do Ahead:
Thaw meat for fajita on Tuesday.

WEEK 7 TUESDAY DINNER MENU

Choose breakfast, lunch and snack items similar to examples in Week 1 and 2.

Menu	Serving Sizes		
	1200 cal. 33 gms. fat	1500 cal. 42 gms. fat	1800 cal. 50 gms. fat
*Fajita Pita	1 serv.	1 1/2 serv.	2 serv.
Chopped Lettuce and Tomato	2 c.	2 c.	2 c.
Peach Sauce and Bananas	1/2 c.	1/2 c.	1 c.
Skim Milk	1 c.	1 c.	1 c.

Do Ahead:
Thaw ground beef for Wednesday.

WEEK 7 WEDNESDAY DINNER MENU

Choose breakfast, lunch and snack items similar to examples in
Week 1 and 2.

Menu	Serving Sizes		
	1200 cal. 33 gms. fat	**1500 cal.** 42 gms. fat	**1800 cal.** 50 gms. fat
Broiled Hamburger	2 oz.	3 oz.	3 oz.
on a Bun	1/2	1	1
*Five Bean Sweet			
and Sour Salad	6 TB.	3/4 c.	1 1/2 c.
Fresh Pear	1	1	2
Skim Milk	1 c.	1 c.	1 c.

Do Ahead:
Thaw ground turkey, pork or beef for meatloaf on Thursday.

WEEK 7 THURSDAY DINNER MENU

Choose breakfast, lunch and snack items similar to examples in
Week 1 and 2.

Menu	Serving Sizes		
	1200 cal. 33 gms. fat	**1500 cal.** 42 gms. fat	**1800 cal.** 50 gms. fat
*Microwave Meatloaf	2 oz.	3 oz.	3 oz.
Baked Potato	1	1	1
Low-fat Margarine	1 tsp.	2 tsp.	4 tsp.
Steamed Peas and Carrots	2 c.	2 c.	2 c.
Strawberries on	1 c.	1 c.	2 c.
Vanilla Ice Milk	none	1/2 c.	1 c.
Skim Milk	1 c.	1 c.	1 c.

Do Ahead:
Thaw meat for taco dish for Friday.

---

* Recipes are included in this book. Check index for page numbers.

WEEK 7 FRIDAY DINNER MENU

Choose breakfast, lunch and snack items similar to examples in Week 1 and 2.

Menu	Serving Sizes		
	1200 cal. 33 gms. fat	1500 cal. 42 gms. fat	1800 cal. 50 gms. fat
*Taco Rice Delight	1/2 serv.	1 serv.	1 1/2 serv.
Chopped Lettuce and Tomatoes	2 c.	2 c.	2 c.
Chunky Fruits in Sugar-Free Ginger Ale	1/2 c.	1/2 c.	1 c.
Skim Milk	1 1/2 c.	1 c.	1 c.

Do Ahead:
Thaw fish for Saturday. Start gazpacho and bread pudding for Saturday.

WEEK 7 SATURDAY DINNER MENU

Choose breakfast, lunch and snack items similar to examples in Week 1 and 2.

Menu	Serving Sizes		
	1200 cal. 33 gms. fat	1500 cal. 42 gms. fat	1800 cal. 50 gms. fat
*My Favorite Gazpacho	3/4 c.	3/4 c.	1 1/2 c.
*Tasty Marinated Grilled White Fish	2 oz.	3 oz.	3 oz.
Steamed Brown Rice	1/3 c.	1/3 c.	2/3 c.
*Miss Pat's Bread Pudding	1/4 serv.	1/2 serv.	1 serv.
Skim Milk	1 c.	1 c.	1 c.

Do Ahead:
Thaw roast and bake cake for Sunday.

WEEK 7 SUNDAY DINNER MENU

Choose breakfast, lunch and snack items similar to examples in Week 1 and 2.

Menu	Serving Sizes		
	1200 cal. 33 gms. fat	1500 cal. 42 gms. fat	1800 cal. 50 gms. fat
*Crockpot Beef Roast	2 oz.	3 oz.	3 oz.
with Fat Free Gravy	1/4 c.	1/4 c.	1/4 c.
Boiled Red Skinned Potatoes	1/2 c.	3/4 c.	1 c.
Steamed Fresh Broccoli	1 c.	1 c.	1 c.
Low-fat Margarine	none	none	2 tsp.
*You'll Love Chutney	6 TB.	3/4 c.	3/4 c.
*Better Than Sex Cake	none	none	1/2 serv.
Skim Milk	1 c.	1 c.	1 c.

Do Ahead:
Thaw chicken for Monday.

WEEK 8 MONDAY DINNER MENU

Choose breakfast, lunch and snack items similar to examples in Week 1 and 2.

Menu	Serving Sizes		
	1200 cal. 33 gms. fat	1500 cal. 42 gms. fat	1800 cal. 50 gms. fat
*Chicken	1/2 serv.	1 serv.	1 serv.
and Noodles in Red Sauce	1/2 c.	1/2 c.	1 1/2 c.
*Tangy Green Beans	1/2 c.	1 c.	1 c.
Fresh Carrot Sticks	1 c.	1 c.	1 c.
Blueberries in Sauce	1/2 c.	1/2 c.	1 c.
Skim Milk	1 c.	1 c.	1 c.

Do Ahead:
Relax!

* Recipes are included in this book. Check index for page numbers.

WEEK 8 TUESDAY DINNER MENU

Choose breakfast, lunch and snack items similar to examples in
Week 1 and 2.

Menu	Serving Sizes		
	1200 cal.	**1500 cal.**	**1800 cal.**
	33 gms. fat	**42 gms. fat**	**50 gms. fat**
*Low-fat Hot Dog	1	2	2
on a Bun	1/2 bun	1 bun	2 buns
*Brussels Sprouts			
Polanaise	1 c.	1 c.	1 c.
Dill Pickle Spears	2	2	2
Chocolate Ice Milk	1/2 c.	1/2 c.	1/2 c.
Cran-raspberry Juice	1/2 c.	1/2 c.	1 c.

Do Ahead:
Relax!

WEEK 8 WEDNESDAY DINNER MENU

Choose breakfast, lunch and snack items similar to examples in
Week 1 and 2.

Check out pages for dinner suggestions from your favorite drive-
through or clean out the refrigerator.

Do Ahead:
Thaw chicken and make pudding for Thursday.

WEEK 8 THURSDAY DINNER MENU

Choose breakfast, lunch and snack items similar to examples in Week 1 and 2.

Menu	Serving Sizes		
	1200 cal. 33 gms. fat	1500 cal. 42 gms. fat	1800 cal. 50 gms. fat
*Cornflake Chicken	2 oz.	3 oz.	3 oz.
*BBQ Baked Potatoes	1/2 c.	1 c	1 1/2 c.
Steamed Sugar Snap Peas	2 c.	2 c.	2 c.
Butterscotch Pudding			
(made with skim milk)	1/2 c.	1/2 c.	1 c.
Skim Milk	1 c.	1 c.	1 c.

Do Ahead:
May put together lasagne for Friday.

WEEK 8 FRIDAY DINNER MENU

Choose breakfast, lunch and snack items similar to examples in Week 1 and 2.

Menu	Serving Sizes		
	1200 cal. 33 gms. fat	1500 cal. 42 gms. fat	1800 cal. 50 gms. fat
*Time Saver Lasagne	1/2 serv.	1 serv.	1 serv.
Fresh Green Salad	2 c.	2 c.	2 c.
No-Oil Dressing	2 tsp.	2 tsp.	2 tsp.
French Bread	1/2 slice	1/2 slice	2 slices
Low-fat Margarine	1 tsp.	1 tsp.	2 tsp.
Melon Wedges	1 c.	1 c.	2 c.
Skim Milk	1 c.	1 c.	1 c.

Do Ahead:
May start chili and make bread for Saturday.

* Recipes are included in this book. Check index for page numbers.

101

WEEK 8 SATURDAY DINNER MENU

Choose breakfast, lunch and snack items similar to examples in
Week 1 and 2.

Menu	Serving Sizes		
	1200 cal. 33 gms. fat	1500 cal. 42 gms. fat	1800 cal. 50 gms. fat
*Cocktail Crab Dip with	2 TB.	1/4 c.	1/4 c.
Vegetable Dippers and	2 c.	2 c.	2 c.
Breadsticks	none	1	2
*Best of Show Chili	3/4 c.	3/4 c.	1 1/2 c.
*Tangy Carrot and			
Raisin Salad	3/4 c.	3/4 c.	3/4 c.
*Poppy Seed Bread	none	1/2 slice	1 slice
Skim Milk	1 c.	1 c.	1 c.

Do Ahead:
May thaw fish and make cake for Sunday.

WEEK 8 SUNDAY DINNER MENU

Choose breakfast, lunch and snack items similar to examples in
Week 1 and 2.

Menu	Serving Sizes		
	1200 cal. 33 gms. fat	1500 cal. 42 gms. fat	1800 cal. 50 gms. fat
*Crusty Fish with Herbs	2 oz.	3 oz.	3 oz.
Baked Potato	1/2	1	1
Low-fat Margarine	1 tsp.	2 tsp.	4 tsp.
*San Francisco Coleslaw	3/4 c.	1 1/2 c.	2 c.
*Raspberry Filled			
Chocolate Cake	1/2 slice	1/2 slice	1 slice
Skim Milk	1 c.	1 c.	1 c.

Do Ahead:
Relax!

WEEK 9 MONDAY DINNER MENU

Choose breakfast, lunch and snack items similar to examples in Week 1 and 2.

Menu	Serving Sizes		
	1200 cal. 33 gms. fat	1500 cal. 42 gms. fat	1800 cal. 50 gms. fat
*Kids Love This			
Cheese Soup	1 c.	1 c.	2 c.
*Hurry Up Sweet and			
Sour Salad	6 TB.	3/4 c.	3/4 c.
Broiled French Bread with	1/2 slice	1 slice	1 slice
Low-fat Margarine	1 tsp.	2 tsp.	2 tsp.
Fresh Banana	1/2	1/2	1
Skim Milk	1 c.	1 c.	1 c.

Do Ahead:
Put casserole together in crockpot for Tuesday.

WEEK 9 TUESDAY DINNER MENU

Choose breakfast, lunch and snack items similar to examples in Week 1 and 2.

Menu	Serving Sizes		
	1200 cal. 33 gms. fat	1500 cal. 42 gms. fat	1800 cal. 50 gms. fat
*Kraut Casserole in			
Crockpot	1 c.	2 c.	2 c.
Rye Bread	1 slice	1 1/2 slices	3 slices
Low-fat Margarine	1 tsp.	2 tsp.	4 tsp.
Apple Slices	1/2 c.	1/2 c.	1 c.
Skim Milk	1 c.	1 c.	1 c.

Do Ahead:
Thaw fish for Tuesday.

* Recipes are included in this book. Check index for page numbers.

WEEK 9 WEDNESDAY DINNER MENU

Choose breakfast, lunch and snack items similar to examples in
Week 1 and 2.

Menu	Serving Sizes		
	1200 cal. 33 gms. fat	1500 cal. 42 gms. fat	1800 cal. 50 gms. fat
*White Fish with Vegetables in the Microwave	1 serv.	1 serv.	1 serv.
Fresh Cherry Tomatoes	1/2 c.	1 c.	1 c.
White Dinner Roll	none	1	2
Low-fat Margarine	none	2 tsp.	4 tsp.
Tropical Fruit Blend	1/2 c.	1/2 c.	1 c.
Skim Milk	1 c.	1 c.	1 c.

Do Ahead:
Thaw ground meat for Thursday.

WEEK 9 THURSDAY DINNER MENU

Choose breakfast, lunch and snack items similar to examples in
Week 1 and 2.

Menu	Serving Sizes		
	1200 cal. 33 gms. fat	1500 cal. 42 gms. fat	1800 cal. 50 gms. fat
*Mexican Corn Main Dish	3/4 c.	1 1/2 c.	1 1/2 c.
Corn Bread Muffin (from a mix)	1/2	1/2	1 1/2
Low-fat Margarine	none	2 tsp.	2 tsp.
Green Grapes	12	12	24
Skim Milk	1 c.	1 c.	1 c.

Do Ahead:
Start soup for Friday.

WEEK 9 FRIDAY DINNER MENU

Choose breakfast, lunch and snack items similar to examples in Week 1 and 2.

Menu	Serving Sizes		
	1200 cal. 33 gms. fat	1500 cal. 42 gms. fat	1800 cal. 50 gms. fat
*Turkey Vegetable Soup	2 c.	2 c.	3 c.
*Salmon Spread for Crackers	2 TB.	1/4 c.	1/4 c.
Low-fat Wheat Crackers	3	6	9
Sherbet	none	1/4 c.	1/2 c.
Skim Milk	1 c.	1 c.	1 c.

Do Ahead:
May prepare cake for Saturday.

WEEK 9 SATURDAY DINNER MENU

Choose breakfast, lunch and snack items similar to examples in Week 1 and 2.

Menu	Serving Sizes		
	1200 cal. 33 gms. fat	1500 cal. 42 gms. fat	1800 cal. 50 gms. fat
*Shrimp Creole	1 c.	2 c.	3 c.
Fresh Green Salad	2 c.	2 c.	2 c.
*Make Your Own Buttermilk Dressing	2 tsp.	2 tsp.	2 tsp.
*Shortcake	1/2 slice	1/2 slice	1 slice
for Strawberries	1 c.	1 c.	2 c.
Skim Milk	1 c.	1 c.	1 c.

Do Ahead:
Thaw chicken, bake cake for Sunday.

---

* Recipes are included in this book. Check index for page numbers.

WEEK 9 SUNDAY DINNER MENU

Choose breakfast, lunch and snack items similar to examples in Week 1 and 2.

Menu	Serving Sizes		
	1200 cal. 33 gms. fat	1500 cal. 42 gms. fat	1800 cal. 50 gms. fat
*Italian Chicken with Cheese	1 serv.	1 serv.	1 serv.
*Fabulous French Bread	none	1/2 slice	1 1/2 slices
*Zucchini with Almonds	1/2 c.	1 c.	1 c.
Lemon Angel Cake with Walnuts	none	1/2 slice	1 slice
Skim Milk	1 c.	1 c.	1 c.

Do Ahead:
Create your own plan for next Monday! You have had nine weeks of practice.

* * * * *

FAST FOOD PICKUP

Use the following menu suggestions at dinner time in your favorite fast food restaurant. The menus represent 25 to 30% calories from fat. Combine these dinner suggestions with the breakfast and lunch menus for approximately 1200, 1500 or 1800 total daily calories.

Burger King

Use with 1200 cal. plan	Cal.	Fat (gms.)	*Use with 1500 cal. plan*	Cal.	Fat (gms.)	*Use with 1800 cal. plan*	Cal.	Fat (gms.)
Chef Salad	178	9	BK Broiler			Hamburger	222	11
Orange Juice	82	0	(no sauce)	289	8	Chocolate Shake	326	10
			Side Salad	25	0	Orange Juice	82	0
			1/3 pkg. Newman's Own					
Total	279	11	Light Italian Drsg.	58	6	Total	630	21
			Orange Juice	82	0			
			Total	454	14			

Dairy Queen

	Cal.	Fat		Cal.	Fat		Cal.	Fat
1/2 order Hot Dog			Single Hamburger	360	16	Fish Sandwich	400	17
with Chili	160	10	Sm. Mr. Misty	190	0	DQ Sandwich	140	4
Small Sundae	210	4				Sm. Mr. Misty	190	0
			Total	550	16			
Total	270	14				Total	30	21

KFC (formerly Kentucky Fried Chicken)

	Cal.	Fat		Cal.	Fat		Cal.	Fat
1/2 order Original			Original Recipe			Original Recipe		
Recipe Center			Center Breast	283	15	Center Breast	283	15
Breast	140	7	Mashed Potatoes			Mashed Potatoes		
Mashed Potatoes			and Gravy	71	2	and Gravy	71	2
and Gravy	71	2	Soft Drink	140	0	Corn on the Cob	176	3
Corn on the Cob	176	3				Soft Drink	140	0
Diet Soft Drink	0	0	Total	494	17			
						Total	670	20
Total	387	12						

McDonalds

	Cal.	Fat		Cal.	Fat		Cal.	Fat
Hamburger	255	9	McLean Deluxe with			McLean Deluxe	320	10
Side Salad	30	1	Cheese	370	14	Small Fries	220	12
1/4 pkg. Reduced			Van. Low-Fat			Van. Low-Fat		
Cal. Red French			Frozen Yogurt			Shake	290	1
Drsg.	40	2	Cone	105	1			
Orange Juice	80	0				Total	830	23
			Total	475	15			
Total	405	12						

Use with 1200 cal. plan	Cal.	Fat (gms.)
1 sl. Medium Cheese and Vegetable		
Pan Pizza	245	9
Fresh Veg. Salad	25	0
1 TB. Reduced Cal.		
Salad Drsg.	20	2
Soft Drink	140	0
Total	**430**	**11**

Use with 1500 cal. plan	Cal.	Fat (gms.)
Pizza Hut		
1 sl. Medium Pan Super		
Supreme Pizza	281	13
Fresh Veg. Salad	25	0
1 TB. Reduced Cal.		
Salad Drsg.	20	2
Soft Drink	140	0
Total	**466**	**15**

Use with 1800 cal. plan	Cal.	Fat (gms.)
2 sl. Medium Cheese Thin and Crispy		
Pizza	398	17
Fresh Veg. Salad	25	0
1 TB. Reduced Cal.		
Salad Drsg.	20	2
Soft Drink	140	0
Total	**583**	**19**

	Cal.	Fat
Small Club Salad	244	12
2 oz. Lite Italian		
Drsg.	23	0
Soft Drink	140	0
Total	**407**	**12**

Subway	Cal.	Fat
6 inch Roast Beef		
Submarine Sand.	344	12
Soft Drink	140	0
Total	**484**	**12**

	Cal.	Fat
12 inch Turkey Breast Breast Sub-		
marine Sand.	644	19
Coffee	0	0
Total	**644**	**19**

	Cal.	Fat
Bean Burrito	197	6
1/2 Apple Grande	123	4
Sugar Free		
Soft Drink	0	0
Total	**320**	**10**

Taco John's	Cal.	Fat
Taco with Chicken	140	9
Refried Beans	331	6
Sugar Free Soft Drink	0	0
Total	**471**	**15**

	Cal.	Fat
Soft Shell Taco		
with Chicken	180	8
Chicken Burrito	227	10
Soft Drink	140	0
Total	**547**	**18**

	Cal.	Fat
Grilled Chicken	100	3
on a Kaiser Bun	200	3
Mustard	4	0
Lemonade	90	0
Total	**394**	**6**

Wendy's	Cal.	Fat
Chili	220	7
Baked Potato	270	0
Iced Tea	0	0
Total	**490**	**7**

	Cal.	Fat
Jr. Hamburger	260	9
Garden Salad	277	5
2 TB. Reduced Cal.		
Italian Drsg.	25	2
Total	**702**	**16**

* * * * *

GRAB-A-SNACK LIST

The daily menu plans include room for your favorite snack choices. A low-fat diet promotes a "grazing" (or frequent feeding) style of eating. This is because the fatty component in foods takes longer to be digested than carbohydrate and protein. The traditional high fat meal promotes a feeling of fullness. As we reduce the fat in our meals, we experience true hunger between meals. Frequent eating does not have to be a problem. You can respond to true hunger between meals with a sensible snack.

A good choice of snack is one that is low in fat, yet satisfies your hunger and provides some vitamins, minerals, or protein. It is essential to keep a variety of sensible snacks on hand at home. Consider this extensive list of snacks. Some contain large amounts of regular sugar and are not indicated for individuals with diabetes. Other snacks are high in sodium and are not meant for people with high blood pressure.

Crunchy Snacks	Cal.	Fat gms.	Sodium mg.	Chol. mg.	Exchange Diets
Apple, 1 whole	81	<1	0	1	1 fruit
Asparagus, 1 c. raw pieces	30	<1	2	0	1 vegetable
Wheat toast, 1 slice with 1 tsp. jam	80	1	140	<5	1 starch
Breadsticks, 1 oz.	86	<1	444	0	1 starch
Broccoli, 1 c. flowerets	46	<1	16	0	1 vegetable
Carrots, 1 raw	31	<1	25	0	1 vegetable
Cauliflower, 1 c. flowerets	24	<1	35	0	Free
Celery, 1 stalk	6	1	90	0	1 starch
Graham crackers, 3 squares	80	1	90	0	1 starch
Finn Crisp crackers, 4	80	0	28	N/A	1 starch
Ideal Crisp Bread, 4	68	0	158	N/A	1 starch
Kavli Norwegian Thick Crackers, 2	70	0	64	N/A	1 starch
Matzo crackers, 1 oz.	115	2	N/A	0	1 1/2 starch
Melba rounds, 5 pieces	50	1	N/A	N/A	1 starch
Oyster crackers, 24	72	1	264	N/A	1 starch
Wasa crackers, 1 piece	44	0	66	N/A	1/2 starch
Saltines, 6	72	1	252	0	1 starch
Kohlrabi, 1 c.	38	<1	28	0	1 vegetable
Green pepper, 1 c. of slices	24	<1	4	0	1 vegetable
Dill pickle, 1 large	6	0	300	0	Free

Crunchy Snacks *Continued*	Cal.	Fat gms.	Sodium mg.	Chol. mg.	Exchange Diets
Popcorn popped in oil, 3 c.	103	4	0	0	1 starch, 1 fat
Popcorn, air-popped, 3 c.	67	0	0	0	1 starch
Popcorn, microwave light variety, 4 c.	104	4	290	0	1 starch, 1 fat
Radishes, 1 c.	14	<1	16	0	1 vegetable

Chewy Snacks

Dried apple slices, 4 pieces	60	<1	21	0	1 fruit
Fruit roll-up, 1/2 oz. roll	50	<1	5	0	1 fruit
Dried apricots, 7 pieces	60	<1	3	0	1 fruit
Bagel, 2 halves toasted	150	1	320	0	2 starch
English muffin, 2 halves toasted	140	2	180	N/A	2 starch
Cheese pizza with veggies, 1/8th med. pie	164	5	309	N/A	1 starch, 1 meat, 1 fat
Raisins, 2 TB.	60	0	0	4	1 fruit
Rice cake, 1 piece	35	0	0	0	1/2 starch
Flour tortilla, 1 sm. broiled with 1/2 tsp. margarine and sprinkled with chili powder	72	3	N/A	N/A	1/2 starch, 1/2 fat

Savory or Salty Snacks

Bean dip, 1/4 c. with raw veggies	90	6	N/A	0	1 fat, 1/2 starch
Lean roast beef, 1 oz.	40	2	560	N/A	1 meat
Cheese, such as Lite Line or Weight Watchers, 1 oz.	50	2	410	N/A	1 meat
Mozzarella cheese, 1 oz. part-skim	80	5	190	16	1 meat
Chicken, white meat canned, 1/4 c.	45	1	115	N/A	1 fat
Crab, 3 oz.	60	<1	270	N/A	1 meat
Taco sauce, 1/4 c. as a dip with raw veggies	15	0	440	0	Free
Ham, 95% lean, 1 oz.	29	1	349	13	1 meat
Pretzels, 1 oz.	110	2	470	0	1 1/2 starch
Tuna, 1/4 c. packed in water	30	<1	155	15	1 meat
Turkey, 1 oz. white meat without skin	51	2	12	21	1 meat

Sweet Snacks

Cinnamon bagel, 2 halves toasted	166	1	320	0	2 starch
Banana, 1 - 9 inch whole	105	<1	0	1	2 fruit

Sweet Snacks Continued	Cal.	Fat gms.	Sodium mg.	Chol. mg.	Exchange Diets
Blueberries, 3/4 c. fresh	61	<1	69	0	1 fruit
Angel food cake, 1/12 cake	140	0	130	0	2 starch
Chocolate angel food cake, 1/12 cake	140	0	300	0	2 starch
Confetti angel food cake, 1/12 cake	140	0	310	0	2 starch
Lemon custard angel food cake, 1/12 cake	140	0	210	0	2 starch
Strawberry angel food cake, 1/12 cake	140	0	160	0	2 starch
Life Savers hard candy, 1 piece	10	0	0	0	Free
Jellied candy, 1 oz.	100	0	10	0	1 1/2 fruit
Licorice, 1 oz.	100	<1	95	0	1 1/2 fruit
Bran or corn flaked cereal, 1 oz.	90	1	150	0	1 starch
Bing cherries, 12	60	2	1	0	1 fruit
Animal crackers, 7 pieces	80	2	87	0	1 starch
Molasses cookies, 1	65	2	65	N/A	1 starch
Vanilla wafers, 6	110	4	70	N/A	1 starch, 1 fat
Chunky fruit in juice, 1/2 c.	50	0	10	0	1 fruit
Sugar free gelatin, 1/2 c.	4	0	35	0	Free
Grapes, 15	60	0	6	0	1 fruit
Cone for sherbet, 1	20	0	35	0	Free
Sherbet, 1/4 c.	55	<1	N/A	N/A	1 starch
Jelly or jam, 2 tsp.	35	0	0	0	1/2 fruit
Kiwifruit, 1 lg.	55	<1	4	0	1 fruit
Melon, 1 cup chunks or balls	55	<1	53	0	1 fruit
Nectarine, 1 fresh	67	<1	0	0	1 fruit
Orange, 1 fresh	65	<1	0	0	1 fruit
Peach, 1 large fresh	60	<1	0	0	1 fruit
Pear, 1 fresh	60	<1	1	0	1 fruit
Pineapple, 3/4 c. fresh or 1/2 c. canned in juice	60	<1	1	0	1 fruit
Sugar free pudding, 1/2 c.	70	0	65	N/A	1 starch
Plums, 2 fresh	60	0	0	0	1 fruit
Raspberries, 1 c. fresh	60	0	0	0	1 fruit
Strawberries, 1 1/4 c. fresh	60	0	1	0	1 fruit

Chocolate Snacks

	Cal.	Fat gms.	Sodium mg.	Chol. mg.	Exchange Diets
Cocoa Krispies cereal, 1 oz. dry	110	0	190	101	1 starch
Chocolate nonfat milk, 1 c.	140	<1	155	5	1 fruit, 1 skim milk
Alba Fit and Frosty, 1 serving	76	<1	206	0	1 skim milk
Chocolate Malt Flavor Carnation Instant Breakfast made with 1 c. skim milk	215	2	285	5	2 fruit, 2 skim milk
Chocolate Pudding Pop, 1	80	2	80	1	1 starch

Frozen or Creamy Snacks	Cal.	Fat gms.	Sodium mg.	Chol. mg.	Exchange Diets
Fruit and Creme Bar,					
1 serving	90	1	20	N/A	1 1/2 fruit
Sorbet, 1/4 c.	60	1	6	0	1 starch
Lemon Frozen Fruit Bar					
(such as Shamitoffs), 1	50	<1	1	0	1 fruit
Fruit and Juice Bar					
(such as Dole), 1	70	<1	6	0	1 fruit
Popsicle, 1	60	<1	0	0	1 fruit
Ice milk, 1/2 c.	110	3	N/A	N/A	1 fat,
					1 starch
Sherbet, 1/4 c.	60	<1	6	N/A	1 starch
Yogurt, frozen, 1/3 c.	70	<1	34	N/A	1 starch
Applesauce, unsweetened					
with cinnamon, 1/2 c.	53	0	0	2	1 fruit
Cottage Cheese,					
1% fat, 1/4 c.	45	1	185	4	1 meat
Yogurt, nonfat with fruit					
and Nutrasweet, 1 c.	100	<1	120	N/A	1 skim milk
Thirst Quenching Snacks					
Low calorie cranberry					
juice, 1/2 c.	24	0	4	0	Free
Grape juice, 1/3 c. mixed					
with 1 c. sugar free 7 Up	60	0	0	0	1 fruit
Apple cider, 1/2 c.	60	0	0	0	1 fruit
Light beer, 1 can	96	0	7	0	1 starch
Grapefruit juice, 1/2 c.	60	0	2	0	1 fruit
Sugar free lemonade, 1 c.	4	0	0	0	Free
Skim milk, 1 c.	86	<1	126	0	1 skim milk
Orange or pineapple juice,					
1/2 c.	60	0	0	0	1 fruit
Sugar free soft drinks, 1 can	2-12	0	6-95	0	Free
V-8 juice, 6 oz.	35	0	345	0	1 vegetable
Warm Snacks					
Vegetable bouillon, 1 packet					
Herb Ox Low Sodium	11	<1	10	0	Free
Oatmeal, 1/2 c. no salt added	69	1	1	0	1 starch
Coffee or decaffeinated					
coffee, 1 c.	5	0	1	0	Free
Tea or herb tea	2	0	0	0	Free
Vegetable beef soup, 1 c.	150	2	1140	N/A	1 starch,
					1 vegetable
Chicken noodle soup, 1 c.	120	4	980	N/A	1 starch,
					1 fat
Hot tomato juice, 6 oz.	30	0	550	0	1 vegetable

BREAKFAST

Breakfast in the Car
Yield: 1 serving

* * *

> 1 pita pocket
> 1 TB. reduced fat cream
>   cheese
> 1/2 c. fresh or dried fruit of
>   choice
> 1 TB. chopped walnuts

Stuff pita pocket with cream cheese, fruit and nuts. Place on a paper napkin and microwave on high power for 20 seconds. Pick up and eat on the go.

Calories per serving: 187
Fat: 7 gm. Cholesterol: 4 mg.
Sodium: 154 mg.
For exchange diets, count:
1 bread/starch, 1 fruit, 1 fat

"Hands on" preparation time: 3 min.

This recipe is suited only for the microwave.

BREAKFAST SCONES
YIELD: 8 SCONES

* * *

Try this English tradition.

> 2 c. "light" baking mix (such
> as Bisquick Light®)
>
> 1/2 c. buttermilk
>
> 1 egg or 1/4 c. liquid egg
> substitute
>
> 2 TB. sugar
>
> 1/4 currants or chopped
> raisins
>
> 1 egg, beaten
>
> Jelly or jam of choice

Preheat oven to 425°. Combine the baking mix, buttermilk, egg, sugar and currants in a large mixing bowl. Turn onto a floured surface and work the dough smooth, forming into a well-rounded lump about the diameter of a large grapefruit. Cut into 8 pie-shaped wedges and place on an ungreased cookie sheet. Brush with beaten egg. Bake for 10 minutes, or until lightly browned. Serve with jam.

Calories per serving: 134
Fat: 3 gm. Cholesterol: 35 mg. with egg;
less than 1 mg. with substitute
Sodium: 297 mg.
For exchange diets, count:
1 bread/starch, 1 fat

"Hands on" preparation time: 15 min.
Baking time: 8 min.

CRANAPPLE BREAKFAST CAKE
YIELD: 12 SERVINGS

* * *

1/3 c. cottage cheese
2 TB. margarine
2 c. light baking mix (such as Bisquick Light®)
1/3 c. skim milk
8 oz. whole cranberry sauce
1 apple, peeled and chopped fine
1 TB. brown sugar
1 TB. cinnamon

Glaze:
1 c. powdered sugar
1 TB. milk
1 TB. cranberry juice
1 tsp. margarine, melted

Preheat oven to 425° F. Blend cottage cheese until smooth.
Transfer to a mixing bowl. Add the margarine and baking mix, and
mix until crumbly. Blend in the milk and stir to form a biscuit
dough. Turn onto a floured surface and roll out into a 12 by 8 inch
rectangle. Turn this onto a no-stick cookie sheet. In the same bowl,
combine the cranberry sauce, apple, sugar and cinnamon. Spread
down the center 4 inches of the dough. Make 2-inch slits at 1-inch
intervals down the sides of the dough. Fold the strips over the
filling. Bake for 12 to 15 minutes. Combine the ingredients for the
glaze and drizzle over the warm cake.

Calories per serving: 166
Fat: 4 gm. Cholesterol: 6 mg.
Sodium: 243 mg.
For exchange diets, count:
1 bread/starch, 1 fruit, 1 fat

"Hands on" preparation time: 20 min.
Baking time: 15 min.

Ham and Cheese Braid for Brunch
Yield: 6 servings

* * *

This recipe is adapted from the National Egg Cooking Contest winner.

1/2 c. chopped green onions	1 (10 oz.) pkg. broccoli, thawed and drained
1/2 cup red or green pepper, chopped	2 oz. part-skim Swiss or cheddar cheese, shredded
1 TB. margarine	2 tsp. lemon juice
6 eggs or 1 1/2 c. liquid egg substitute	1 (10 oz.) tube refrigerated pizza crust
1/4 c. skim milk	1 egg
1/4 tsp. salt	1 TB. water
1/2 tsp. basil	Poppy seeds
4 oz. lean ham, diced	

Preheat oven to 375° F. In large skillet over medium heat, cook onion and red pepper in margarine, until tender but not brown. Beat together eggs, milk, salt and basil until blended. Stir in ham. Pour over onion and peppers in the pan. Gently scramble until eggs are thick, but still moist. Remove from heat and set aside. In medium bowl, toss together broccoli, cheese and lemon juice. Set aside. Unroll dough onto a baking sheet that has been sprayed with nonstick cooking spray. Pat to form a rectangle. Spread egg mixture in a 3-inch wide strip down length of dough. Top with broccoli mixture. Make cuts in dough at 1-inch intervals on both sides of rectangle, just to edge of filling. Fold dough strips over filling to make a braided appearance. In small bowl, beat together 1 egg with water. Brush top of dough with egg mixture. Sprinkle with poppy seeds. Bake for 25 minutes, or until golden brown. Cut into 4 slices.

Calories per serving: 240
Fat: 14 gm. Cholesterol: 288 mg. with egg; 51 mg. with substitute
Sodium: 682 mg.
(To reduce sodium, substitute chopped turkey for ham.)
For exchange diets, count:
2 lean meat, 1 fat, 1 bread/starch

"Hands on" preparation time: 20 min.
Baking time: 25 min.

Lemon Breakfast Ring
Yield: 18 slices

* * *

1 pkg. dry yeast
1 c. warm water
3 1/4 c. sifted flour
1/4 c. margarine
1 c. sugar
1/2 tsp. salt
1/2 tsp. nutmeg
2 TB. grated fresh lemon peel
4 eggs, unbeaten or 1 c. liquid
   egg substitute

Mix yeast and warm water; stir in one cup of the flour. Set in warm place. Meanwhile, in a large mixing bowl, cream margarine, sugar, salt and flavorings until fluffy. Beat in eggs, one at a time. Stir in yeast mixture and the rest of the flour, beating smooth at low speed. Pour into a tube pan that has been sprayed with nonstick cooking spray. Allow to rise in a warm place, until batter is about 1 inch from top of pan. Preheat oven to 375° F. Bake for 50 minutes, or until it tests done. Cool in pan. Turn out onto a serving platter.

Calories per serving: 174
Fat: 4 gm. Cholesterol: 60 mg. with egg; 0 mg. with substitute
Sodium: 105 mg.
For exchange diets, count:
1 1/2 bread/starch, 1 fat

"Hands on" preparation time: 15 min.
Rising time: 30 min.
Baking time: 50 min.

LOW-FAT FRENCH TOAST
YIELD: 4 SERVINGS, 2 SLICES EACH

* * *

8 slices bread
(Best French toast will be
from bread that has been
allowed to dry out)
2 eggs or 1/2 c. liquid egg
substitute
1/2 c. skim milk
1/2 tsp. vanilla
1 tsp. oil

In a shallow bowl, mix egg, milk and vanilla with a fork until smooth. Pour oil into a no-stick skillet and heat over medium-high flame. Use a pastry brush, if necessary, to coat surface of pan with oil. Reduce heat to medium. Dip the bread into the egg mixture and place in skillet. Brown both sides of bread and top with your choice of sugar-free fruit preserves (recommended for diabetics) or maple syrup.

Calories per serving: 193
Fat: 5 gm. Cholesterol: 137 mg. with egg;
less than 1 mg. with substitute
Sodium: 358 mg.
For exchange diets, count:
2 bread/starch, 1 fat
(Nutrient analysis does not include topping.)

"Hands on" preparation and cooking time: 20 min.

LOW-FAT PANCAKES
YIELD: 4 SERVINGS, 2 PANCAKES EACH

* * *

1 1/2 c. light baking mix (such
  as Bisquick Light®)
1 egg or 1/4 c. liquid egg
  substitute
1/2 c. milk
1/2 tsp. vanilla
1 tsp. oil

No-stick skillet is necessary for this recipe.

In a mixing bowl, mix baking mix with egg, milk, and vanilla
until smooth. Pour oil into a no-stick skillet and heat over
medium-high flame. Use a pastry brush, if necessary, to coat
surface of pan with oil. Reduce heat to medium. Pour 1/4 c. of
batter into skillet and cook until bubbles form. Turn pancake
and brown on other side. Top with your choice of sugar-free fruit
preserves (recommended for diabetics) or maple syrup.

Calories per serving: 142
Fat: 6 gm. Cholesterol: 69 mg. with egg;
less than 1 mg. with substitute
Sodium: 220 mg.
For exchange diets, count:
1 bread/starch, 1 fat
(Nutrient analysis does not include topping.)

"Hands on" preparation and cooking time: 20 min.

Old-Fashioned Coffeecake with Dried Apricots
Yield: 12 servings

* * *

1 c. oatmeal	1 c. dried apricots, finely chopped
1/4 c. melted margarine	
1/3 c. chopped almonds	*Glaze:*
1/3 c. brown sugar	1/4 c. powdered sugar
1 egg, beaten slightly or 1/4 c. liquid egg substitute	1 TB. orange juice concentrate
3/4 tsp. almond extract	
1 lb. frozen bread dough, thawed at room temperature	

Spray a baking sheet with nonstick cooking spray. Combine oatmeal and margarine in a large mixing bowl. Stir in almonds, sugar, egg and almond extract. Spread thawed dough out into a rectangle on baking sheet. Spread oatmeal mixture down the center. Sprinkle with chopped apricots. On each side of filling, cut slits in dough and fold over, making a braid pattern. Allow to rise for 30 minutes in a warm place. Bake for 30 minutes, or until golden brown. Mix powdered sugar and orange juice concentrate together. Drizzle over warm coffeecake and serve.

Calories per serving: 193
Fat: 6 gm. Cholesterol: 23 mg. with egg; 0 mg. with substitute
Sodium: 232 mg.
For exchange diets, count:
2 bread/starch, 1 fat

"Hands on" preparation time: 15 min.
Rising time: 30 min.
Baking time: 30 min.

OVERNIGHT BREAKFAST PIE
YIELD: 8 SERVINGS

* * *

4 eggs or 1 c. liquid egg
substitute

2 1/2 c. frozen hash brown
potatoes

4 oz. reduced fat Swiss
cheese, shredded

1/2 c. lowfat cottage cheese

1/3 c. skim milk

1 green onion, thinly sliced

1/4 tsp. salt

1/4 tsp. pepper

4 drops hot pepper sauce

4 oz. lean ham, chopped into
small pieces

1/2 c. corn flake crumbs

In a medium mixing bowl, beat eggs until foamy. Stir in
remaining ingredients, except crumbs. Pour into a 9-inch pie pan
that has been sprayed with nonstick cooking spray. Sprinkle
with crumbs. Cover and refrigerate overnight. Preheat oven to
325° F. Bake for 50 minutes or until knife inserted near the
center comes out clean. To microwave, cook on 80% power for 15
to 18 minutes or until eggs are set.

Calories per serving: 246 mg.
Fat: 9 gm. Cholesterol: 152 mg. with egg; 17 mg. with substitute
Sodium: 492 mg.
(To reduce sodium, substitute cooked chopped turkey for the ham.)
For exchange diets, count:
1 1/2 bread/starch, 1 1/2 lean meat, 1 fat

"Hands on" preparation time: 15 min.
Baking time: conventional oven, 50 min.; microwave, 18 min.

Quiche without the Crust
Yield: 8 slices

* * *

> 4 slices bacon, diced
>
> 1 c. reduced fat Swiss cheese, shredded
>
> 1/3 c. chopped green onion
>
> 1/4 c. diced green pepper,
>
> 1 (4 oz.) can mushroom pieces, drained or 1/2 c. sliced fresh mushrooms
>
> 2 1/4 c. skim milk
>
> 1 c. "light" baking mix (such as Bisquick Light®)
>
> 2 eggs, beaten well
>
> 1/4 tsp. pepper

Preheat oven to 400° F. Dice bacon onto a microwave tray. Cover with a paper towel and cook on high power for 3 minutes. Drain. Spray a 9-inch pie plate with nonstick cooking spray. Sprinkle bacon pieces, shredded cheese, onion, green pepper, and mushrooms over the pie plate. Beat the remaining ingredients until smooth, in the blender or with the electric mixer. Pour into pie. Bake for 30 minutes, or until eggs are set.

Calories per serving: 135
Fat: 5 gm. Cholesterol: 80 mg. with eggs; 11 mg. with substitute
Sodium: 406 mg.
(To reduce sodium, reduce bacon.)
For exchange diets, count:
1 bread/starch, 1 fat

"Hands on" preparation time: 10 min.
Baking time: 30 min.

Sportsman's Breakfast
Yield: 1 serving

* * *

An early morning treat for bikers, hikers or people who go fishing.

> 1 English muffin
> 1 oz. lean ham, cut into 2 slices
> 2 slices pineapple
> 2 thin slices tomato
> 1 oz. reduced fat Swiss cheese, cut into 2 slices

Split the English muffin in half. Layer ham, pineapple, tomato and cheese. Broil for 4 minutes under medium flame, until cheese melts and edges of muffin are toasted.

Calories per serving: 245
Fat: 9 gm. Cholesterol: 28 mg.
Sodium: 784 mg.
(To reduce sodium, substitute lean roast beef for ham.)
For exchange diets, count:
2 meat, 1 bread/starch, 1 fruit

"Hands on" preparation time: 7 min.
Broiling time: 4 min.

BREADS, MUFFINS, BISCUITS

Aloha Loaf
Yield: 1 loaf or 18 slices

* * *

> 1/4 c. margarine
> 1 c. sugar
> 2 eggs or 1/2 c. liquid egg
>   substitute
> 1/4 c. buttermilk
> 1/2 c. mashed banana
> 1 (7 oz.) can crushed
>   pineapple in juice
> 2 c. flour
> 1/2 tsp. soda
> 1 tsp. baking powder
> 1/4 tsp. salt
> 1/2 c. maraschino cherries,
>   chopped

Preheat oven to 350° F. In a large mixing bowl, cream margarine and sugar. Beat in eggs, one at a time. Combine the banana and buttermilk in a small cup. In a separate small bowl, stir together the flour, soda, baking powder and salt. Add the flour mixture alternately with the banana and buttermilk mixture to the egg mixture. Fold in chopped cherries. Pour into an ungreased loaf pan. Bake for 50 to 55 minutes or until a toothpick inserted into the loaf returns clean.

Calories per serving: 143
Fat: 3 gm. Cholesterol: 30 mg. with egg; 0 gm. with substitute
Sodium: 142 mg.
For exchange diets, count:
1 bread/starch, 1/2 fruit and 1/2 fat

"Hands on" preparation time: 15 min.
Baking time: 50 min.

BANANA BREAKFAST MUFFINS
YIELD: 1 DOZEN

* * *

1/2 c. mashed banana
1/2 c. milk
1 egg or 1/4 c. liquid egg
   substitute
2 c. light baking mix (such as
   Bisquick Light®)
1/4 c. sugar
1/2 tsp. cinnamon

Preheat oven to 400° F. Blend banana, milk and egg with a fork
in a mixing bowl. Stir in remaining ingredients, just until
moistened. Line muffin cups with papers and fill 2/3 full. Bake
for 15 minutes, or until evenly browned.

Calories per serving: 96
Fat: 2 gm. Cholesterol: 23 mg. with egg;
less than 1 mg. with substitute
Sodium: 198 mg.
For exchange diets, count:
1 bread/starch, 1/2 fat

"Hands on" preparation time: 10 min.
Baking time: 15 min.

BEER AND CHEESE BISCUITS
YIELD: 12

* * *

> 2 c. light baking mix (such as
> Bisquick Light®)
> 1/2 c. finely chopped green
> onion
> 1 TB. margarine
> 1/2 c. shredded part-skim
> cheddar cheese
> 2/3 c. beer

Preheat oven to 400° F. Mix together the baking mix, onion and
cheese in large bowl. Use a pastry blender to cut in shortening.
Add beer and stir just until blended. Drop by spoonfuls onto
baking sheet that has been sprayed with nonstick cooking spray.
Bake for 12 minutes, or until golden brown.

Calories per serving: 91
Fat: 3 gm. Cholesterol: 3 mg.
Sodium: 218 mg.
For exchange diets, count:
1 bread/starch, 1/2 fat

"Hands on" preparation time: 15 min.
Baking time: 12 min.

CARROT AND ORANGE ZUCCHINI BREAD
YIELD: 2 LOAVES OR 36 SLICES

* * *

3 eggs or 3/4 c. liquid egg
   substitute
1/2 c. vegetable oil
1/2 c. orange juice
1 tsp. orange extract
2 tsp. vanilla extract
1/2 c. sugar
1 TB. cinnamon
3 c. flour
1/2 tsp. salt
1/2 tsp. baking powder
2 c. finely grated zucchini
1/2 c. finely grated carrot or
   1/2 c. baby food strained
   carrots

Preheat oven to 350° F. In a large mixing bowl, beat first five
ingredients until smooth. Beat in sugar. In a small mixing bowl,
combine dry ingredients and blend well. Add to egg mixture and
stir smooth. Fold in zucchini and carrots. Spray two loaf pans
with nonstick cooking spray. Pour batter into the pans and bake
for 1 hour, or until bread tests done.

Calories per serving: 85
Fat: 3 gm. Cholesterol: 23 mg. with egg; 0 mg. with substitute
Sodium: 79 mg.
For exchange diets, count:
1 bread/starch, 1/2 fat

"Hands on" preparation time: 20 min.
Baking time: 1 hr.

CRUNCHY RAISIN BRAN BREAD
YIELD: 1 LOAF OR 18 SLICES

* * *

1 1/8 c. flour
6 TB. oatmeal
6 TB. brown sugar
1/4 c. bran cereal
2 tsp. baking powder
1 TB. cinnamon
1/4 tsp. salt
3/4 c. skim milk
1 egg or 1/4 c. liquid egg
   substitute
1/4 c. vegetable oil
1/2 c. raisins

Crunchy Topping:
1/4 c. oatmeal
2 TB. brown sugar
1 tsp. margarine

Preheat oven to 375° F. In a large mixing bowl, mix dry ingredients well. In another small bowl, beat together milk, eggs and oil. Pour into dry ingredients and mix just until moistened. Stir in raisins and spoon into a loaf pan that has been sprayed with nonstick cooking spray. In a small bowl, mix ingredients for topping until crumbly. Sprinkle over batter. Bake for 45 minutes, or until it tests done. Cool in pan, then remove and slice.

Calories per serving: 112
Fat: 3 gm. Cholesterol: 15 mg. with egg; less than 1 mg. with substitute
Sodium: 122 mg.
For exchange diets, count:
1 bread/starch, 1/2 fat

"Hands on" preparation time: 15 min.
Baking time: 45 min.

Dr. Downey's Whole Grain Quick Bread
Yield: 1 loaf or 18 slices

* * *

1 c. flour
1 tsp. soda
1 tsp. baking powder
2 tsp. sugar
1/4 tsp. salt
2 TB. margarine
1/4 c. oatmeal
2 c. whole wheat flour
1 1/2 c. buttermilk

Preheat oven to 375° F. In a large mixing bowl, combine first five ingredients. Cut in margarine. Stir in oatmeal and whole wheat flour. Add buttermilk; then use a dough hook to knead until smooth; or knead smooth by hand on a floured board. Form dough into a 7-inch circle. Make two crosses across the loaf. Bake for 40 minutes, or until browned.

Calories per serving: 109
Fat: 2 gm. Cholesterol: less than 1 mg.
Sodium: 174 mg.
For exchange diets, count:
1 bread/starch, 1/2 fat

"Hands on" preparation time: 15 min.
Baking time: 40 min.

FABULOUS FRENCH BREAD
YIELD: 2 LOAVES OR 40 SLICES

* * *

2 pkg. dry quick acting yeast
1/2 c. water
1/2 tsp. sugar
2 TB. sugar
2 TB. margarine
2 tsp. salt
2 c. boiling water
7 1/2 c. flour
Cornmeal to dust pans

Dust 2 French bread loaf pans with cornmeal. Dissolve yeast in
1/2 c. water and stir in 1/2 tsp. sugar. Combine 2 TB. sugar,
margarine, salt and boiling water in a large mixing bowl. Cool to
lukewarm and stir in yeast. Slowly add flour, processing with
food processor, or electric mixer, or by hand, until dough is
smooth and elastic. Cover and allow to rise in a warm place until
double in bulk (about 30 minutes). Form into two loaves, and
place in prepared bread pans. Allow to rise 15 minutes. Place a
pan of boiling water in the bottom of the oven. Bake in preheated
400° oven for 20 minutes. Cool for 10 minutes, then remove
loaves from pan and cool on a rack.

Calories per slice: 96
Fat: 1 gm. Cholesterol: 0 mg.
Sodium: 107 mg.
For exchange diets, count:
1 bread/starch.

"Hands on" preparation time: 15 min.
Rising time: 45 min.
Baking time: 20 min.

JUST PEACHY MUFFINS
YIELD: 1 DOZEN

* * *

1/2 c. chopped peaches
1/4 c. sliced almonds
2 TB. brown sugar
1/2 tsp. ground cinnamon
1 1/4 c. flour
1/3 c. sugar
1 TB. baking powder
1/4 tsp. salt
1 c. flaked bran cereal
1 c. skim milk
1 beaten egg, or 1/4 c. liquid
  egg substitute
2 TB. vegetable oil

Preheat oven to 400° F. In a small mixing bowl, stir together peaches, almonds, brown sugar, and cinnamon; set aside. In a large mixing bowl, stir together flour, sugar, baking powder and salt. In a medium mixing bowl, stir together cereal and milk and let stand for 5 minutes. Stir egg and oil into cereal mixture. Add cereal mixture to flour mixture, and stir just until moist. Line 12 muffin cups with paper baking cups. Spoon half of the batter into the cups. Top each with 2 tsp. of peach filling. Spoon remaining batter on top of filling. Bake for 20 minutes until golden.

Calories per serving: 142
Fat: 4 gm. Cholesterol: 23 mg. with egg;
less than 1 mg. with substitute
Sodium: 226 mg.
For exchange diets, count:
1 bread/starch, 1/2 fruit, 1 fat

"Hands on" preparation time: 15 min.
Baking time: 20 min.

Maple Syrup Muffins
Yield: 12

* * *

3/4 c. bran flakes
1/2 c. skim milk
1/2 c. maple syrup
1 egg, slightly beaten or
1/4 c. liquid egg substitute
2 TB. vegetable oil
1 1/2 c. flour
1 TB. baking powder
1/2 tsp. salt
2 TB. chopped walnuts

Glaze:
1/3 c. powdered sugar
1 TB. maple syrup

Preheat oven to 400° F. Combine cereal, milk and maple syrup in a mixing bowl. Mix in egg and oil. In another bowl, combine remaining ingredients. Add to cereal mixture, stirring until just moistened. Divide batter into 12 greased muffin tins. Bake for 18 to 20 minutes. Combine sugar and syrup for glaze and spoon over warm muffins.

Calories per serving: 156
Fat: 3 gm. Cholesterol: 23 mg. with egg;
less than 1 mg. with substitute
Sodium: 257 mg.
For exchange diets, count:
1 bread/starch, 1/2 fruit, 1 fat

"Hands on" preparation time: 15 min.
Baking time: 20 min.

Poppy Seed Bread
Yield : 2 loaves, or 36 slices

* * *

My dear neighbor, Diane Tisue, invented this.

> 3 c. flour
> 1/2 tsp. salt
> 1 1/2 tsp. baking powder
> 1 1/2 c. sugar or substitute
> 2 tsp. vanilla
> 1 1/2 c. skim milk
> 3/4 c. vegetable oil
> 1/2 c. frozen orange juice
>   concentrate, thawed
> 2 TB. poppy seeds
> 3 eggs or 3/4 c. liquid egg
>   substitute
> 1 1/2 tsp. almond extract
> 2 TB. powdered sugar
> 1 TB. finely grated orange
>   rind

Preheat oven to 350° F. Put all ingredients, except powdered sugar and orange rind, into a bowl. Beat for 2 minutes. Divide between 2 loaf pans and bake for 55 minutes. Remove from pan and sprinkle with powdered sugar and grated orange rind while warm.

Calories per 1 slice serving: 125
Fat: 5 gm. Cholesterol: 22 mg. with egg
Sodium: 31 mg.
For exchange diets, count:
1 bread/starch and 1 fat.

"Hands on" preparation time: 20 min.
Baking time: 55 min.

RAISIN BREAD IN THE MICROWAVE
YIELD: 1 ROUND LOAF OR 18 SLICES

* * *

12 oz. warm beer
2 c. self-rising flour
4 TB. margarine, melted
3 TB. sugar
1/2 c. chopped raisins
1 TB wheat germ

Combine first four ingredients in a large mixing bowl. Beat until smooth. Fold in raisins. Sprinkle wheat germ on the bottom of a round microwave-safe dish. Pour batter into pan. Sprinkle wheat germ on top. Microwave on 70% power for 5 minutes. Turn pan. Microwave 6 to 7 more minutes, or until batter is set. Cool slightly, then remove from pan and continue cooling bread on a rack.

Calories per serving: 98
Fat: 3 gm. Cholesterol: 0 mg.
Sodium: 170 mg.
For exchange diets, count:
1 bread/starch, 1/2 fat

"Hands on" preparation time: 10 min.
Baking time: 12 min.

STRAWBERRY SURPRISE MUFFINS
YIELD: 1 DOZEN

* * *

> 1 pkg. "light" bran muffin mix
> 3/4 c. strawberry preserves

Preheat oven as directed on muffin mix package. In a small mixing bowl, mix bran muffin mix as directed. Spoon half of batter into prepared muffin cups. Top with 1 TB. of strawberry preserves. Spoon remaining batter over preserves. Bake as directed.

Calories per serving: 112
Fat: 4 gm. Cholesterol: 23 mg. with egg;
less than 1 mg. with substitute
Sodium: 122 mg.
For exchange diets, count:
1 bread/starch, 1 fat

"Hands on" preparation time: 10 min.
Baking time: 15 to 20 min.

SALADS

ALISON'S STRAWBERRY SALAD
YIELD: *4 SERVINGS, 3/4 CUP EACH*

* * *

This one is a favorite of my 12-year-old neighbor.

1 pkg. plain gelatin (such as
  Knox®)
8 oz. can crushed pineapple
1 c. plain low-fat yogurt
10 oz. package frozen
  strawberries, drained

Drain pineapple and pour juice into a 1-quart glass microwave-
safe salad bowl. Stir gelatin into juice and microwave on high
power for 45 seconds, just until gelatin is dissolved. Stir in
yogurt, strawberries and reserved pineapple. Chill for at least 2
hours.

Calories per serving: 86
Fat: 0 gm. Cholesterol: 0 mg.
Sodium: 165 mg.
For exchange diets, count:
1 fruit

"Hands on" preparation time: 10 min.
Chilling time: 2 hr.

CABBAGE SALAD WITH POPPY SEED DRESSING
YIELD: 4 SERVINGS, 1 1/2 CUPS EACH

* * *

1 head green cabbage,
shredded

1 large carrot, shredded or
may substitute 1 lb. bag
shredded cabbage and
carrots

1 red or green pepper, finely
chopped

Dressing:

1/3 c. sugar or equivalent in
sugar substitute

1 TB. vegetable oil

1/2 c. vinegar

1/4 tsp. salt

2 tsp. dry mustard

2 tsp. poppy seeds

1/4 c. evaporated skim milk

Combine cabbage, carrots and pepper in a salad bowl. Mix ingredients for the dressing in a shaker container. Pour over vegetables. Serve.

Calories per serving: 133
Fat: 4 gm. Cholesterol: less than 1 mg.
Sodium: 173 mg.
For exchange diets, count:
2 vegetable, 1 fat, 1/2 fruit

"Hands on" preparation time: 10 min.

Carrot Marinade
Yield: 8 servings, 3/4 cup each

* * *

1 1/2 lb. carrots, cut into coins 1/2 green pepper, chopped fine 1 scallion, sliced fine 8 oz. no-added-salt tomato   sauce 1/4 c. vinegar 2 TB brown sugar 1 tsp. prepared mustard 1/2 tsp. celery seed 1 TB. Worcestershire sauce

Place sliced carrots and 1 TB. water into microwave-safe 2-quart dish. Cover with plastic wrap and microwave on high for 3 minutes. Drain well. Transfer carrots to a 2-quart salad bowl. Add green pepper and scallion. Combine tomato sauce, vinegar, brown sugar, mustard, Worcestershire sauce, and celery seed in a shaker container and pour over vegetables, tossing to coat. This salad keeps well in the refrigerator for 4 days.

Calories per serving: 77
Fat: less than 1 gm. Cholesterol: 0 mg.
Sodium: 71 mg.
For exchange diets, count:
1 bread/starch

"Hands on" preparation time: 15 min.

Crunchy Broccoli Salad
Yield: 8 servings, 1 cup each

* * *

> 1 lg. bunch of fresh broccoli,
>   chopped into bite-sized
>   pieces
> 1 small red onion, sliced thin
> 4 strips bacon, broiled crisp
>   and crumbled
> 1/2 c. raisins
> 1/2 c. chopped walnuts
>
> *Dressing:*
> 1/3 c. reduced-calorie
>   mayonnaise
> 1/2 c. plain nonfat yogurt
> 1/4 c. sugar or substitute
> 2 TB. vinegar

Mix together broccoli, onion, bacon, raisins and walnuts in a
salad bowl. These ingredients will keep covered in the
refrigerator for 4 days. Combine ingredients for dressing in
shaker container. Pour over broccoli just before serving. Toss
and serve.

Calories per serving: 178
With sugar substitute: 154
Fat: 4 gm. Cholesterol: 14 mg.
Sodium: 135 mg.
For exchange diets, count:
3 vegetables, 1/2 bread/starch, 1 1/2 fat.
With sugar substitute, count:
3 vegetables, 1 1/2 fat.

"Hands on" preparation time: 15 min.

Guilt-free Potato Salad
Yield: 4 servings, 1 cup each

* * *

> 5 medium potatoes
> 2 eggs, hard boiled and
>   chopped
> 1/3 c. chopped onion
> 1 c. chopped celery
> 1 c. nonfat mayonnaise (such
>   as Kraft Free®)
> 2 TB. vinegar
> 1 tsp. salt
> 1 tsp. sugar
> 1/4 tsp. white pepper

Wash, peel, and cube potatoes. Place in 3-quart microwave dish
with 2 TB. of water. Cover and cook on high power for 6 minutes.
Drain in colander and cover with 6 ice cubes to speed cooling.
While potatoes are cooking, boil eggs for 10 minutes. While eggs
are cooking, combine mayonnaise, vinegar, salt, sugar, pepper,
onion and celery in a 3-quart salad bowl. When eggs are finished
cooking, rinse under cold water, peel and chop into dressing
mixture. Add cooled potatoes, stir just to blend and serve.

Calories per serving: 275
Fat: 4 gm. Cholesterol: 274 mg.
Sodium: 193 mg.
For exchange diets, count:
3 bread/starch, 1 fat
Nutrient Alert: To reduce cholesterol, use white of egg only.

"Hands on" preparation time: 20 min.

Hurry Up Sweet 'n Sour Vegetable Salad

Yield: 8 servings, 3/4 cup each

* * *

2 c. very finely chopped celery
1 large onion, chopped fine
20 oz. pkg. frozen mixed
   vegetables, thawed and
   drained

Dressing:
3/4 c. sugar or equivalent in
   substitute
1/2 c. vinegar
1 TB. flour
1 TB. prepared mustard

Combine celery, onion and drained vegetables in a 2-quart bowl.
Combine sugar, vinegar, flour and mustard in a small saucepan.
Bring to a boil and boil for 1 minute. Cool. IMPORTANT: If
using Equal® brand sugar substitute, do not cook; add to the
cooled dressing. Pour over the vegetables and chill. This salad
keeps very well in the refrigerator for up to 1 week.

Calories per serving: 132 with sugar, 60 with substitute
Fat: 1 gm. Cholesterol: 0 mg.
Sodium: 31 mg.
For exchange diets, count:
2 vegetables, 1 fruit.
If using sugar substitute, count just 2 vegetables.

"Hands on" preparation time: 15 min.

Make Your Own Buttermilk Ranch Dressing
Yield: 2 cups or 16 servings, 2 TB. each

* * *

> 1 c. buttermilk
> 1 c. nonfat mayonnaise (such as Kraft Free®)
> 1/2 tsp. salt
> 2 tsp. monosodium glutamate or Accent®
> 1 TB. dried parsley
> 1/4 tsp. white pepper
> 1 tsp. garlic powder
> 1 tsp. onion powder

Measure ingredients into a blender container. Process until smooth. Transfer to covered dressing jar and refrigerate. Great as topping on baked potatoes or as dressing on green salad.

Calories per serving: 6
Fat: less than 1 gm. Cholesterol: less than 1 mg.
Sodium: 248 mg.
For exchange diets, count:
2 TB. as a FREE FOOD
Nutrient Alert: To reduce sodium, reduce monosodium glutamate and salt.

"Hands on" preparation time: 10 min.

OLD FASHIONED CUCUMBERS
YIELD: 4 SERVINGS, 1 CUP EACH

* * *

> 1 qt. fresh cucumbers, peeled
> and sliced thin
> 1 medium onion, cut into
> slices
> 1 tsp. salt
> 1/4 c. sugar
> 1/4 c. vinegar
> 1/2 tsp. celery seed

Wash and prepare cucumbers and onion; layer into a shallow bowl. Sprinkle with salt and cover with one tray of ice cubes. Allow to marinate for at least 30 minutes. Drain well, using your hands to squeeze the water out of cucumbers and onions. Transfer cucumbers and onions to a serving bowl. Combine vinegar, sugar and celery seed in a shaker container. Pour over vegetables, cover, and chill.

Calories per serving: 73
Fat: 0 gm. Cholesterol: 0 mg.
Sodium: 61 mg.
For exchange diets, count:
1 vegetable, /2 fruit.

"Hands on" preparation time: 10 min.
Chilling time: 30 min.

Pina Colada Fruit Salad
Yield: 4 servings, 1 cup each

* * *

1/4 c. shredded coconut
1 c. low-fat banana yogurt
1/4 c. pineapple juice
2 tsp. rum extract
1 TB. coconut cream
  (optional)
3 c. fresh or canned fruit of
  choice (I prefer a mixture of
  pineapple, banana, oranges
  and kiwi)

Combine coconut, yogurt, pineapple juice, rum extract, and coconut cream in a small glass bowl. Stir to blend. Fold in fresh or canned fruits just before serving.

Calories per serving: 150
Fat: 2 gm. Cholesterol: 14 mg.
Sodium: 58 mg.
For exchange diets, count:
2 fruit, 1/2 fat

"Hands on" preparation time: 10 min.

Salads

Red and Green Pea Salad
Yield: 4 servings, 1 cup each

* * *

> 1/2 c. nonfat mayonnaise
> (such as Kraft Free®)
>
> 1/4 c. reduced-fat Italian
> salad dressing
>
> 16 oz. pkg. frozen peas,
> thawed and drained
>
> 1 c. chopped celery
>
> 2 slices bacon, cooked and
> crumbled
>
> 1/4 c. chopped red onion

Combine mayonnaise and Italian salad dressing in a salad bowl.
Add remaining ingredients and mix lightly. Serve.

Calories per serving: 110
Fat: 4 gm. Cholesterol: 2 mg.
Sodium: 189 mg.
For exchange diets, count:
1 bread/starch, 1 fat

"Hands on" preparation time: 15 min.

San Francisco Coleslaw
Yield: 4 servings, 1 1/2 cups each

* * *

Tastes great with fish.

---

1 head green cabbage,
   shredded
1 large carrot, shredded or
   may substitute a 1 lb. bag
   shredded cabbage and
   carrots
1/2 medium red onion,
   chopped
1/4 c. raisins

Dressing:
1 1/2 tsp. prepared mustard
1/4 c. sugar or equivalent in
   sugar substitute
1 TB. oil
1/4 tsp. salt
2 TB. vinegar
1/2 tsp. celery seed

Combine vegetables with raisins in a salad bowl. In a shaker container, combine all ingredients for the dressing and shake well. Pour dressing over vegetables and mix. The mixed salad with dressing will keep in the refrigerator for 8 hours. The dressing will keep by itself for 2 weeks in the refrigerator.

Calories per serving: 139
Fat: 4 gm. Cholesterol: 0 mg.
Sodium: 156 mg.
For exchange diets, count:
3 vegetable, 1 fat, 1/2 fruit

"Hands on" preparation time: 15 min.

SWEET AND SOUR BEAN SALAD
YIELD: 8 SERVINGS, 1 CUP EACH

* * *

1 lb. fresh green beans
1/2 c. diced celery
1/2 c. chopped red onion
15 oz. can kidney beans,
  rinsed and drained
15 oz. can garbanzo beans,
  rinsed and drained
1/2 c. cider vinegar
1/2 c. apple juice
3 TB. sugar
2 TB. prepared mustard
1 TB. cornstarch
1/4 tsp. pepper

Wash and stem green beans, cutting them into small pieces.
Bring 1 quart of water to a boil in a 3-quart saucepan. Add beans
and cook for 15 minutes, or until tender. Drain, rinse under cold
water, and drain again. Transfer to a large salad bowl. Add next
four ingredients to the salad bowl. Toss gently. Combine
vinegar, apple juice, sugar, mustard, cornstarch and pepper in a
small saucepan. Cook for 5 minutes, or until thickened. Pour
over bean mixture and toss. Chill and serve.

Calories per serving: 124
Fat: 6 gm. Cholesterol: 0 mg.
Sodium: 215 mg.
For exchange diets, count:
1 bread/starch, 1 fat

"Hands on" preparation time: 15 min.
Cooking time: 20 min.

TANGY CARROT AND RAISIN SALAD
YIELD: 4 SERVINGS, 3/4 CUP EACH

* * *

2 c. shredded carrots
1/2 c. minced green pepper
1/3 c. raisins
1 TB. minced onion
1 small apple, cored and
  shredded
2 TB. cider vinegar
1 TB. vegetable oil
2 tsp. sugar or equivalent
  sugar substitute
1/4 tsp. celery seeds
1/4 tsp. dry mustard

In medium-sized salad bowl, combine first five ingredients. In shaker container, combine remaining ingredients. Pour dressing over salad just before serving.

Calories per serving: 119
Fat: 4 gm. Cholesterol: 0 mg.
Sodium: 154 mg.
For exchange diets, count:
1 fruit, 1 vegetable, 1 fat

"Hands on" preparation time: 15 min.

VEGETABLE RELISH
YIELD: 4 SERVINGS, 3/4 CUP EACH

* * *

1 c. shredded carrots
1 c. chopped cucumber
1/2 c. chopped red pepper
1/4 c. finely chopped red onion
3 TB. cider vinegar
1 tsp. sugar
1/4 tsp. salt
1 TB. vegetable oil

Combine carrot, cucumber, pepper and onion in a medium bowl.
Set aside. Stir together vinegar, sugar and salt. Whisk in oil.
Pour over vegetables and toss to coat. Cover and refrigerate at
least 1 hour before serving. This is a great accompaniment to
grilled fish.

Calories per serving: 84
Fat: 4 gm. Cholesterol: 0 mg.
Sodium: 162 mg.
For exchange diets, count:
2 vegetable, 1 fat.

"Hands on" preparation time: 15 min.

MAIN DISH SALADS

CREOLE SHRIMP SALAD
YIELD: 4 SERVINGS, 2 CUPS EACH

* * *

1 lb. shrimp, peeled and deveined	1/4 c. chopped celery
2 c. quick rice, uncooked	1/4 c. chopped green onion
2 c. water	3 TB. red wine vinegar
14 oz. can no-added-salt chunky tomatoes, drained or 1 1/2 c. chopped fresh tomato	1/2 tsp. thyme
	1/4 tsp. hot pepper sauce (such as Tabasco®)
	1/8 tsp. salt
1 green pepper, seeded and chopped	1/4 tsp. pepper
	2 TB. parsley

Bring 3 quarts of water to boiling. Add the shrimp and return to a boil. Boil for 1 minute. Drain the shrimp. Immediately rinse with cold water and drain again. While the shrimp are cooking, combine rice and water in 3-quart microwave dish. Cover and microwave the rice on high power for 5 minutes. While the rice is cooking, chop celery, pepper and onion. In a 3 -quart salad bowl, combine tomatoes, wine vinegar, thyme, and seasonings. To speed cooling of rice, add 6 ice cubes, then drain well. Stir cooled shrimp and rice into tomato mixture. Garnish with parsley and serve.

Calories per serving: 285
Fat: 1 gm. Cholesterol: 64 mg.
Sodium: 200 mg.
For exchange diets, count:
2 bread/starch, 2 lean meat, 1 vegetable

"Hands on" preparation time: 15 min.

GREEK TUNA AND PASTA SALAD
YIELD: 4 SERVINGS, 1 CUP EACH

* * *

1/2 c. orzo or other small
pasta
2 (6 1/2 oz.) cans tuna packed
in water, drained
2 oz. feta cheese, crumbled
2 medium tomatoes, peeled
and chopped
2/3 c. reduced-calorie herb
vinaigrette dressing

Cook pasta according to package directions, rinse under cold water, and drain. In large salad bowl, gently toss pasta with remaining ingredients. Cover and chill until serving time.

Calories per serving: 250
Fat: 9 gm. Cholesterol: 50 mg.
Sodium: 498 mg.
For exchange diets, count:
1 bread/starch, 3 lean meat

"Hands on" preparation time: 15 min.

NOT JUST ANOTHER CHICKEN SALAD
YIELD: 4 SERVINGS, 1 CUP EACH

* * *

1/3 c. picante sauce
1/2 c. reduced-calorie
  mayonnaise
1 TB. honey
1 c. diced cooked chicken
1 c. thinly sliced celery
1 c. seedless grapes, halved
2 TB. chopped almonds or
  pecans
1/4 c. sliced scallions

Combine picante sauce, mayonnaise and honey in a 3-quart salad bowl. Mix well. Stir in chicken, celery, grapes, and almonds. Cover and chill in freezer for 10 minutes. Sprinkle with scallions to garnish and serve.

Calories per serving: 163
Fat: 9 gm. Cholesterol: 30 mg.
Sodium: 197 mg.
For exchange diets, count:
1 lean meat, 1 fat, 1 fruit

"Hands on" preparation time: 20 min.

POTATO, BACON AND GREEN BEAN SUPPER SALAD

YIELD: 4 SERVINGS, 1 1/2 CUPS EACH

* * *

8 small new potatoes, sliced
1/2 lb. green beans, cut into
    1-inch pieces
1/4 c. white vinegar
1 TB. vegetable oil
1/4 tsp. pepper
4 strips bacon, diced
2 green onions, thinly sliced
3 TB. red wine vinegar
2 TB. sherry
2 tsp. sugar

Place potatoes and green beans in a microwave dish. Sprinkle with 2 TB. water. Cover and cook on high power for 5 minutes, or until tender. Transfer to a large bowl. Sprinkle with white vinegar, oil and pepper. In a heavy skillet, cook diced bacon and onions until crisp. Drain off liquid. Add red wine vinegar, sherry and sugar to the skillet. Boil 1 minute. Pour over potatoes and green beans in the salad bowl. Toss and serve.

Calories per serving: 313
Fat: 5 gm. Cholesterol: 5 mg.
Sodium: 120 mg.
For exchange diets, count:
3 bread/starch, 1 vegetable, 1 fat

"Hands on" preparation time: 15 min.

SALMON PASTA SALAD WITH CUCUMBER DRESSING
YIELD: 4 SERVINGS, 2 CUPS EACH

* * *

1 lb. canned salmon
1 tsp. lemon juice
1/2 c. reduced-calorie creamy
cucumber dressing
1 large cucumber, peeled,
seeded and chopped fine
8 oz. rotelle or spiral-shaped
pasta
Fresh salad greens

Drain salmon; remove skin and bones. Place in 3-quart salad bowl, sprinkle with lemon juice, and place in the refrigerator. Cook pasta according to package directions, rinse under cold water, and then drain well. Prepare cucumber and add to salmon; then add drained pasta and dressing. Stir well and serve on a bed of fresh salad greens.

Calories per serving: 344
Fat: 7 gm. Cholesterol: 44 mg.
Sodium: 518 mg.
For exchange diets, count:
2 bread/starch, 3 lean meat, 1 vegetable

"Hands on" preparation time: 15 min.

Turkey and Vegetable Salad
Yield: 4 servings, 1 1/2 cups each

* * *

4 lg. red-skinned potatoes	1 TB. dried parsley or 3 TB. fresh
2 TB. water	1 TB. dried chives or 3 TB. fresh
1 lb. green beans, cut into 1-inch pieces	1 tsp. celery seed
1 qt. water	1/2 tsp. dry mustard
2 c. cooked turkey, cut into bite-sized pieces	1/4 tsp. salt
	1/4 tsp. white pepper
1 stalk celery, diced	Celery leaves as garnish
1/2 c. plain yogurt	
1/4 c. light mayonnaise	

Wash and slice potatoes into a 2-quart microwave dish. Sprinkle
with 2 TB. water, cover, and microwave on high power for 5
minutes, turning once during cooking. Drain potatoes after
cooking and place in a large salad bowl. Meanwhile, bring 1
quart of water to a boil in a 3-quart saucepan. Add beans and
cook 15 minutes, or until tender. Drain beans, rinse with cold
water and drain again. Add beans, turkey and celery to the salad
bowl. In another small bowl, combine all remaining ingredients,
except celery leaves. Toss dressing with turkey and vegetables
just before serving. Garnish with celery leaves.

Calories per serving: 356
Fat: 3 gm. Cholesterol: 46 mg.
Sodium: 253 mg.
For exchange diets, count:
3 bread/starch, 1 vegetable, 2 lean meat

"Hands on" preparation time: 35 min.

SOUPS

Beefy Mushroom & Barley Soup
Yield: 8 servings, 2 cups each

* * *

2 1/2 c. sliced mushrooms
1/2 c. chopped onion
2 TB. margarine
1/3 c. flour
6 c. water
1 lb. lean stew beef cubes
2 c. skim milk
1/2 c. quick pearled barley
1 TB. dry sherry
2 tsp. Worcestershire sauce
1 TB. dried parsley or 3 TB.
  minced fresh parsley
1/4 tsp. pepper

In a 2-quart kettle, simmer 1 pound stew beef in 6 cups water for 15 minutes. In skillet, sauté mushrooms and onion in margarine. Stir in flour and gradually add milk, stirring thick. Transfer this to the kettle of beef and stock, stirring to blend. Stir in barley and seasonings. Simmer for 15 minutes. This may be prepared and frozen for later use.

Calories per 1 c. serving: 253
Fat: 9 gm. Cholesterol: 29 mg.
Sodium: 126 mg.
For exchange diets, count:
3 lean meat, 1 1/2 bread starch.

"Hands on" preparation time: 10 min.
Cooking time: 30 min.

Best of Show Chili
Yield: 8 servings, 1 1/2 cups each

* * *

> 1 lb. lean ground beef
> 1 tsp. oregano
> 1/2 tsp. thyme
> 1 large onion, chopped
> 1 green pepper, chopped
> 1/2 tsp. monosodium
>   glutamate
> 2 cloves garlic, minced
> 1 TB. paprika
> 1 TB. chili powder
> 1 tsp. cumin
> 2 (16 oz.) cans no-added-salt
>   chunky tomatoes
> 2 (16 oz.) cans kidney beans
> 8 oz. no-added-salt tomato
>   sauce
> 1/2 oz. unsweetened
>   chocolate, grated

Brown ground beef in a Dutch oven and drain well. Add next 9 ingredients and cook over medium heat for 8 minutes, stirring, until vegetables are cooked through. Add chunky tomatoes, beans, and tomato sauce. Bring mixture to a boil. Stir in shredded unsweetened chocolate. Reduce heat and simmer for at least 20 minutes.

Calories per serving: 242
Fat: 8 gm. Cholesterol: 42 mg.
Sodium: 318 mg.
For exchange diets, count:
2 lean meat, 1 bread/starch, 2 vegetable

"Hands on" preparation time: 15 min.
Cooking time: 20 min.

Chicken Gumbo
Yield: 8 servings, 2 cups each

* * *

2 c. cooked chicken, cut into bite-sized pieces	16 oz. can no-added-salt chunky tomatoes, undrained
1 oz. ham, cut into small pieces	1/8 tsp. pepper
1 TB. vegetable oil	2 TB. minced fresh parsley
1 medium onion, diced	1 bay leaf
1 medium green pepper, chopped	1/2 tsp. thyme
2 ribs celery, sliced	Dash of Worcestershire sauce
4 c. no-added-salt chicken broth	1 c. quick rice, uncooked
	1 c. frozen cut okra
	1/2 tsp. filé powder (optional)

In a large stockpot, sauté chicken and ham in vegetable oil. Add all remaining ingredients except filé powder and bring to a boil. Cover and reduce heat to simmer for 20 minutes. Add filé powder. Remove bay leaf and serve. If you intend to freeze this soup, do not add filé powder. Add it just before serving.

Calories per serving: 144
Fat: 4 gm. Cholesterol: 28 mg.
Sodium: 228 mg.
For exchange diets, count:
1 bread/starch, 1 vegetable, 1 lean meat

"Hands on" preparation time: 15 min.
Cooking time: 20 min.

Chicken Chili Without Tomatoes
Yield: 8 servings, 1 1/2 cups each

* * *

1 1/2 lb. cooked, diced chicken (or 6 chicken breasts, cooked and diced)
1 TB. vegetable oil
1 green pepper, diced
1 red pepper, diced
1 large onion, diced
1 clove garlic, minced
1 jalapeno pepper, seeded and minced
2 tsp. cumin
1 TB. chili powder
1 chicken bouillon cube or 1 tsp. instant bouillon
1 1/2 c. water
1/2 tsp. pepper
16 oz. can white kidney beans, drained
16 oz. package frozen corn

In large stockpot, sauté peppers and onion in oil. Add garlic and jalapeno pepper and cook for 3 minutes, until vegetables are softened. Add cumin, chili powder, bouillon cube, pepper and water. Heat to boiling. Stir in corn and diced cooked chicken. Reduce heat to medium. Cover and simmer for 15 minutes. Add beans toward end of cooking and stir to blend.

Calories per serving: 198
Fat: 5 gm. Cholesterol: 40 mg.
Sodium: 354 mg.
For exchange diets, count:
2 lean meat, 1 bread/starch, 1 vegetable

"Hands on" preparation time: 15 min.
Cooking time: 15 min.

CHILLED CUCUMBER SOUP
YIELD: 4 SERVINGS, 1 CUP EACH

* * *

If you have never tried this, you're missing a special part of summer.

1 1/2 c. pared, seeded, and chopped fresh cucumbers
1 1/2 c. no-added-salt chicken broth
1/4 tsp. salt
1/8 tsp. white pepper
4 drops hot pepper sauce (such as Tabasco®)
2 tsp. lemon juice
1/2 c. 50% reduced-fat sour cream
1/4 c. finely diced cucumber

Combine chopped cucumbers, broth, and seasonings in a blender. Cover and blend until consistency is smooth. Add sour cream to mixture and blend well. Chill for 30 minutes. Garnish with finely diced cucumber.

Calories per serving: 39
Fat: 2 gm. Cholesterol: 6 mg.
Sodium: 142 mg.
For exchange diets, count:
1 vegetable, 1/2 fat

"Hands on" preparation time: 10 min.
Chilling time: 30 min.

HAMBURGER SOUP
YIELD: 4 SERVINGS, 2 CUPS EACH

* * *

> 1/2 lb. lean ground beef
> 1/2 c. chopped onion
> 2 ribs celery, diced
> 1/2 c. fresh mushrooms, sliced thin
> 1 tsp. basil
> 1 tsp. dill weed
> 1/4 tsp. celery salt
> 1 large carrot, sliced thin
> 6 c. no-added-salt chunky tomatoes
> 2 medium potatoes, peeled and cubed

In a large stockpot, brown ground beef with onion, celery and mushrooms. Drain off any fat from meat. Add all remaining ingredients to the stockpot and bring to a boil. Reduce heat to a simmer for 20 minutes, or until carrots and potatoes are tender.

Calories per serving: 250
Fat: 7 gm. Cholesterol: 42 mg.
Sodium: 67 mg.
For exchange diets, count:
2 lean meat, 1 vegetable, 1 1/2 bread/starch

"Hands on" preparation time: 15 min.
Cooking time: 20 min.

KIDS LOVE THIS CHEESE SOUP
YIELD: 4 SERVINGS, 1 CUP EACH

* * *

1/4 c. finely chopped onion
1/4 c. finely chopped carrot
1/4 c. finely chopped celery
1 TB. water
1 TB. margarine
1/3 c. flour
1 1/2 c. no-added-salt chicken broth
2 c. skim milk
4 oz. reduced-fat cheddar cheese, shredded
Paprika as garnish

In microwave dish, combine onion, carrot, celery and 1 TB. water. Cover and microwave on high power for 3 minutes. In 2-quart saucepan, melt margarine, over medium heat; then whisk in flour and then milk, blending until smooth. Add broth, vegetables, and shredded cheese, stirring until cheese melts. Ladle into bowls and garnish with paprika.

Calories per serving: 163
Fat: 7 gm. Cholesterol: 16 mg.
Sodium: 184 mg.
For exchange diets, count:
1 skim milk, 1 bread/starch

"Hands on" preparation time: 15 min.

Mulligatawny Soup
Yield: 4 servings, 2 cups each

* * *

1/4 c. chopped onion
1/2 tsp. curry powder
1 TB. margarine
1 c. cooked, diced chicken
1 small tart apple, peeled, cored
  and chopped
1/2 c. shredded carrot
1/4 c. chopped celery
2 TB. chopped green pepper
3 TB. flour
4 c. no-added-salt chicken broth
16 oz. can no-added-salt chunky
  tomatoes
2 tsp. lemon juice
1 1/2 tsp. dried parsley or 1 1/2
  TB. minced fresh parsley
1 tsp. sugar
2 whole cloves

In a large stockpot, cook onion, and curry powder in margarine until onion is tender. Stir in chicken, chopped apple, carrot, celery and green pepper. Cook, stirring occasionally, for 5 minutes, or until vegetables are tender crisp. Sprinkle flour over chicken mixture and stir to mix well. Stir in all remaining ingredients. Bring to a boil, then reduce heat to simmer 15 more minutes.

Calories per serving: 139
Fat: 4 gm. Cholesterol: 20 mg.
Sodium: 80 mg.
For exchange diets, count:
1 lean meat, 3 vegetable

"Hands on" preparation time: 15 min.
Cooking time: 20 min.

MY FAVORITE GAZPACHO
YIELD: 8 SERVINGS, 3/4 CUPS EACH

* * *

4 lg. ripe tomatoes, peeled,
    seeded, and chopped
1 c. no-added-salt-tomato juice
1 c. chopped peeled cucumber
1 red bell pepper, chopped
2 tsp. chopped jalapeno
    pepper
1/4 c. chopped scallions
2 TB. red wine vinegar
1 large clove garlic, minced or
    1/2 tsp. garlic powder
1/4 tsp. salt (optional)
1 tsp. sugar or substitute

Combine all ingredients and marinate in the refrigerator for 2
hours. Serve as a salad or use as a dip with tortillas. To make a
crunchy low-fat tortilla, spray flour tortillas with shortening,
sprinkle with chili powder, then bake at 200° F. for 15 minutes
and cool. Gazpacho keeps well for 3 days in the refrigerator.

Calories per serving: 75
Fat: 4 gm.   Cholesterol: 0 mg
Sodium: 80 mg. with salt; 19 mg. without salt
For exchange diets, count:
2 vegetable, 1 fat.

"Hands on" preparation time: 15 min.

Pumpkin Soup
Yield: 4 servings, 1 1/2 cups each

* * *

1 TB. margarine
1 c. chopped onion
1/2 c. diced celery
1 clove garlic, minced or
  1/4 tsp. garlic powder
1/4 tsp. salt
1/2 tsp. white pepper
3 c. no-added-salt chicken
  broth
16 oz. can solid pack pumpkin
1 c. evaporated skim milk
2 scallions, finely chopped

In 2-quart saucepan, melt margarine. Add onion, celery and garlic, cooking until vegetables are soft. Add broth, salt and pepper and simmer for 15 minutes. Stir in pumpkin and evaporated skim milk. Cook over medium flame (being careful not to boil) for 5 minutes, then pour into a blender container and blenderize on low speed, about 30 seconds, until creamy. Ladle into soup bowls. Top with chopped scallions, and serve.

Calories per 1 1/2 c. serving: 120
Fat: less than 1 gm. Cholesterol: 2 mg.
Sodium: 215 mg.
For exchange diets, count:
1 bread/starch, 2 vegetable.

"Hands on" preparation time: 15 min.
Cooking time: 20 min.

Turkey Vegetable Soup
Yield: 4 servings, 2 cups each

* * *

1 tsp. vegetable oil
1 c. sliced zucchini
1 c. sliced mushrooms
1 clove garlic, minced
2 potatoes, peeled and cubed
1 c. cooked and diced turkey
1 c. carrots, sliced thin
2 tsp. cumin
1/4 tsp. salt
1 c. green beans
1 1/2 c. no-added-salt chunky
   tomatoes
1 c. no-added-salt chicken
   broth
1/2 tsp. pepper

Heat oil in large stockpot. Add zucchini, mushrooms and garlic. Sauté for 5 minutes over medium-high heat. Add all remaining ingredients to the stockpot. Bring to a boil, then reduce heat to simmer for 20 minutes, or until potatoes and carrots are tender.

Calories per serving: 214
Fat: 2 gm. Cholesterol: 20 mg.
Sodium: 205 mg.
For exchange diets, count:
1 lean meat, 1 bread/starch, 3 vegetable

"Hands on" preparation time: 15 min.
Cooking time: 25 min.

Winter in New England Clam Chowder
Yield: 4 servings, 2 cups each

* * *

3 large red-skinned potatoes, peeled
  and cubed
2 TB. water
3 slices bacon, cut into small pieces
1 medium onion, chopped
2 TB. flour
1/4 tsp. thyme
1/4 tsp. pepper
8 oz. can clam broth
1 c. evaporated skim milk
2 c. skim milk
6 1/2 oz. can minced clams, drained
  and liquid reserved
3 to 4 drops hot pepper sauce (such
  as Tabasco®)

Place cubed potatoes and 2 TB. water in microwave dish. Cover and cook on high power for 5 minutes, turning dish once during cooking. Meanwhile, cook bacon in 2-quart stockpot until crisp. Drain away grease. Add onion to pan and sauté for 3 minutes, or until soft. Stir in flour, thyme, and pepper. Add steamed potato cubes, reserved canned clam liquid, bottled clam broth, evaporated skim milk and skim milk. Bring just to a boil, stirring mixture. Reduce heat and stir in clams and red pepper sauce. Cook for more 2 minutes.

Calories per serving: 287
Fat: 4 gm. Cholesterol: 21 mg.
Sodium: 488 mg.
For exchange diets, count:
1 skim milk, 1 lean meat, 2 bread/starch
Nutrient Alert: To reduce sodium, omit bacon.

"Hands on" preparation time: 20 min.

CASSEROLES

Bean Casserole Olé
Yield: 8 servings, 1 1/2 cups each

* * *

---

4 strips bacon, broiled crisp
2 TB. margarine
1 c. chopped onion
1 green pepper, diced
2 (15 oz.) cans kidney or pinto
    beans, drained
4 tsp. chili powder
1 tsp. garlic powder
1 tsp. dried jalapeno pepper
    (optional)
14 oz. can chopped tomatoes
    or 2 c. fresh tomatoes
2 oz. part-skim American
    cheese, shredded
2 oz. part-skim Monterey jack
    cheese, shredded

Broil bacon until crisp and crumble. Set aside. Melt margarine in a small skillet over medium flame; sauté onion and pepper until tender. Combine the sautéed vegetables, beans, seasonings and tomatoes in a 3-quart baking dish. Stir well. Bake for 35 minutes at 350° F. Sprinkle with cheeses and bacon and bake for 5 more minutes. Serve. Leftovers freeze well.

Calories per serving: 349
Fat: 11 gm. Cholesterol: 28 mg.
Sodium: 392 mg.
For exchange diets, count:
2 bread/starch, 2 lean meat, 1 vegetable, 1 fat

"Hands on" preparation time: 15 min.
Baking time: 40 min.

Baked Burrito
Yield: 8 servings, 8 oz. each

* * *

> 8 (10 inch) flour tortillas
> 1 lb. lean ground beef
> 4 oz. part-skim American
> cheese, shredded
> 1/4 c. chopped scallions
>
> *Mexican Sauce:*
> 8 oz. no-added-salt tomato
> sauce
> 1/4 tsp. garlic powder
> 1/2 tsp cumin
> 1/8 tsp. cayenne powder
> (optional)
> 1/2 tsp. dried jalapeno
> peppers (optional)
> 1 TB. lemon juice
> 1 TB. sugar

Brown and drain the ground beef. Meanwhile, shred the cheese and chop the onions. Mix the sauce ingredients together and pour over drained beef, stirring to mix. Place 1/2 c. beef in each tortilla, fold and place seam side down on a baking sheet. Top with cheese and scallions. Bake 15 minutes at 350° F. Serve with lettuce and tomatoes. These burritos freeze well on sheets or in baking dishes.

Calories per serving: 212
Fat: 6 gm. Cholesterol: 57 mg.
Sodium: 180 mg.
For exchange diets, count:
2 lean meat, 1 bread starch and 1 vegetable.

"Hands on" preparation time: 20 min.
Baking time: 15 min.

Broccoli Rice Casserole
Yield: 8 servings, 1 1/2 cups each

* * *

1/2 c. diced celery .
1/2 c. chopped onion
1/2 lb. fresh mushrooms,
   sliced
2 TB. margarine
2 (10 oz.) pkgs. frozen
   chopped broccoli, thawed
1 c. quick rice, uncooked
2 oz. Light American cheese,
   shredded
2/3 c. Mary's Cream Soup
   Substitute (check index for
   page number of recipe)

In a no-stick skillet, sauté onion, celery and sliced mushrooms in margarine until tender. Using 1 large or 2 small casserole dishes, combine sauteed vegetables with broccoli, rice and shredded cheese. Combine 2/3 c. Mary's Cream Soup Substitute with 2 1/2 c. water in a shaker container. Add to the other ingredients and mix well. Bake at 350° F. for 30 minutes or microwave on high power for 15 to 18 minutes, until mixture is bubbly.

Calories per serving: 132
Fat: 5 gm.   Cholesterol: 4 mg.
Sodium: 302 mg.
For exchange diets, count:
1 bread/starch, 1 vegetable, 1 fat.

"Hands on" preparation time: 15 min.
Baking time: conventional oven, 30 min.; microwave oven, 18 min.

California Blend Vegetables with Chicken and Rice
Yield: 4 servings

* * *

> 1 1/2 c. water
>
> 1 1/2 c. quick rice, uncooked
>
> 1/2 lb. skinless, boned chicken, cut into strips
>
> 1 tsp. vegetable oil
>
> 10 oz. reduced fat cream of chicken soup (such as Campbells' Healthy Request®)
>
> 1 c. skim milk
>
> 2 TB. prepared mustard
>
> 2 oz. part-skim Swiss cheese, shredded
>
> 16 oz. package frozen California Blend® vegetables (or use a combination of carrots, cauliflower and broccoli)

Combine water and quick rice in a 3-quart microwave dish. Cover and microwave on high power for 5 minutes. Meanwhile, using a 3-quart deep skillet or Dutch oven, sauté chicken strips in oil until lightly browned. Stir in soup, milk, mustard and cheese. Bring to a full boil. Stir in vegetables. Return mixture to a boil, then reduce heat and continue cooking until vegetables are tender crisp. Pour chicken and vegetable mixture over rice and serve.

Calories per serving: 422
Fat: 9 gm. Cholesterol: 80 mg.
Sodium: 508 mg.
For exchange diets, count:
2 bread/starch, 2 vegetables, 1/2 skim milk, 3 lean meat

"Hands on" preparation time: 20 min.

CROCKPOT POTATOES AND HAM
YIELD: 4 SERVINGS, 2 CUPS EACH

* * *

1 lb. frozen hashbrowns or 4
   large potatoes, peeled and
   cubed

1/4 c. chopped onion

1 c. buttermilk

1/2 c. soft cheddar cheese
   spread (such as Spreadery®
   by Kraft)

10 oz. can reduced fat cream
   of chicken soup (such as
   Campbell's Healthy
   Request®)

8 oz. lean ham, chopped

Mix all ingredients together in a crockpot and cook for 4 hours on
medium heat. To microwave, mix all ingredients except ham in
3-quart microwave dish and cook on 70% power for 12 minutes.
Stop cooking at 4 and 8 minutes to stir well. At 12 minutes, stir
in ham and cook on high power for 2 more minutes.

Calories per serving: 282
Fat: 9 gm. Cholesterol: 35 mg.
Sodium: 722 mg.
(To reduce sodium, use half ham and half turkey.)
For exchange diets, count:
2 bread/starch, 2 lean meat

"Hands on" preparation time: 10 min.
Cooking time: crockpot method, 4 hr.; microwave method, 20 min.

Discover Grits Casserole
Yield: 4 servings, 1 1/2 cups each

* * *

If you haven't cooked with grits, you don't know what you're missing!

> 4 c. water
> 1 1/4 c. quick cooking grits
> 1/2 c. soft cheddar cheese
> spread, such as Spreadery®
> by Kraft
> 1/4 tsp. white pepper
> 1/2 c. milk
> 3 beaten eggs or 3/4 c. liquid
> egg substitute
> 1/2 c. corn flake crumbs

Heat water in 3-quart saucepan to boiling. Stir in grits and salt. Return to boiling; then reduce heat. Simmer for 10 minutes, stirring occasionally. While grits are cooking, combine cheese spread, pepper, milk and beaten eggs in a 3-quart microwave dish. Stir in cooked grits and top with cornflake crumbs. Microwave on 70% power for 8 minutes or until center of mixture is firm. Allow casserole to rest for 5 minutes before serving.

Calories per serving: 178
Fat: 7 gm. Cholesterol: 215 mg. with egg; 10 mg. with substitute
Sodium: 201 mg.
For exchange diets, count:
1 bread/starch, 1 lean meat, 1 fat

"Hands on" preparation time: 15 min.
Cooking time: 8 min.
Resting time: 5 min.

END OF THE MONTH VEGETABLE CASSEROLE
YIELD: 4 SERVINGS, 1 1/2 CUPS EACH

* * *

1/2 lb. lean ground beef
1 small onion, chopped
1 small head of green
  cabbage, shredded
2 carrots, peeled and sliced
  thin
2/3 c. quick rice
13 oz. can reduced sodium
  tomato soup (such as
  Campbell's Healthy
  Request®)
1 1/2 c. water
1 tsp. garlic powder
1/2 tsp. pepper
2 tsp. cumin

Brown ground beef in a small skillet with onion. Drain well.
Combine with all other ingredients in a 3-quart casserole dish.
Bake uncovered for 1 hour at 350° F. or cover and microwave on
high power for 15 to 20 minutes, stopping cooking twice to stir.
Casserole is done when cabbage and carrots are tender.

Calories per serving: 301
Fat: 8 gm. Cholesterol: 42 mg.
Sodium: 499 mg.
For exchange diets, count:
2 bread/starch, 2 vegetable, 2 lean meat

"Hands on" preparation time: 15 min.
Baking time: conventional oven, 1 hr.; microwave oven, 30 min.

Hot Tamale Supper
Yield: 4 wedges

* * *

1 c. yellow cornmeal	3 TB. tomato paste
2 1/2 c. no-added-salt beef broth	1 tsp. oregano
	1/2 tsp. cumin
1 tsp. vegetable oil	1 TB. chili powder
1/4 c. chopped onion	1 1/2 c. corn, drained if canned corn is used
1 clove garlic, minced	
1/2 lb. lean ground beef, browned and drained	1/3 c. raisins
	4 oz. can green chilis, drained and chopped
1 1/2 c. chopped fresh tomatoes or no-added-salt canned chunky tomatoes	
	2 TB. Parmesan cheese, grated

Preheat oven to 350° F. In a large saucepan, combine 1/2 c. broth with the cornmeal. In a separate pan, bring the remainder of the broth to a boil. Stir the broiling broth into the cornmeal. Cover and cook over medium heat, stirring until mixture thickens. Set aside to cool. In a skillet, heat the oil and lightly sauté the onion and garlic. Add the lean ground beef and continue cooking until the meat loses its red color. Drain the meat mixture and return it to the skillet. Add tomatoes, tomato paste, oregano, cumin and chili powder to the beef. Simmer 5 minutes. Stir in corn, raisins and chilis. Remove from heat. Spray a 3-quart casserole dish with nonstick cooking spray. Line the bottom and sides of the dish with the cornmeal mush. Spoon in the filling and sprinkle with Parmesan cheese. Bake for 30 minutes.

Calories per serving: 308
Fat: 10 gm. Cholesterol: 50 mg.
Sodium: 162 mg.
For exchange diets, count:
2 bread/starch, 2 lean meat, 1 vegetable

"Hands on" preparation time: 20 min.
Baking time: 30 min.

Kraut Casserole in the Crockpot
Yield: 4 servings, 2 cups each

* * *

4 strips bacon	1/4 c. brown sugar or equivalent in brown sugar substitute
1 c. chopped onion	
32 oz. jar sauerkraut, drained and rinsed	1/4 tsp. pepper
1 c. peeled and chopped apples	1/4 tsp. thyme
	1/2 c. dry vermouth or dry white wine
1 large potato, peeled and shredded	1/4 lb. lean ham, cut into chunks (or may substitute leftover cooked pork)
1 c. no-added-salt chicken broth	

Snip bacon into small pieces and place on a microwave broiling
rack. Cover with a paper towel and cook on high power for 3
minutes. Drain bacon and place in crockpot. Add all remaining
ingredients. Cook in crockpot for minimum of 4 hours. To
prepare in the microwave, microwave bacon as before, drain and
place in a microwave-safe casserole dish. Add all remaining
ingredients except ham. Cook uncovered on high power for 15
minutes. Add ham. Cook on 50% power for 3 minutes. Serve.

Calories per serving: 263 mg.
Fat: 6 gm. Cholesterol: 24 mg.
Sodium: 920 mg.
(To reduce sodium, substitute cooked pork for ham and/or
fresh cabbage for sauerkraut.)
For exchange diets, count:
1 bread/starch, 1 lean meat, 1 fruit, 3 vegetable

"Hands on" preparation time: 10 min.
Cooking time: crockpot, 4 hr.; microwave, 18 min.

MARY'S CREAM SOUP SUBSTITUTE
YIELD: EQUIVALENT OF 10 CANS OF SOUP

* * *

> 2 c. nonfat dried milk
> 3/4 c. cornstarch
> 1/4 c. chicken or beef bouillon
>   particles
> 2 TB. dried minced onion
> 1 tsp. thyme
> 1 tsp. basil
> 1/2 tsp. pepper

Mix ingredients together and store in a covered container. Use as a substitute for creamed soups in casserole recipes. To use, mix 1 1/4 c. cold water with 1/3 c. of the mix in a small saucepan. Add 1 tsp. margarine. Cook until thickened and substitute for 10 oz. can of cream soup.

Calories per 1/3 c. mix: 94
Fat: 1 gm. Cholesterol: 3 mg.
Sodium: 112 mg.
(To reduce sodium, use low sodium bouillon.)
For exchange diets, count:
1 bread/starch.

"Hands on" preparation time: 10 min.

Mexican Corn Main Dish
Yield: 8 servings, 3/4 cup each

* * *

1 lb. lean ground beef, browned
4 ears fresh corn or
10 oz. package frozen corn,
    thawed
1 egg or 1/4 c. liquid egg
    substitute
1/2 c. nonfat yogurt
1 c. mozzarella cheese, shredded
1/2 c. cornmeal
7 oz. can diced green chilies
1/4 tsp. garlic powder
1/4 tsp. salt
Chopped fresh parsley, as an
    optional garnish

Preheat oven to 350° F. Brown ground beef in a small skillet and
drain well. Spray a 3-quart casserole dish with nonstick cooking
spray. Add ground beef to the casserole dish. Cut the corn off the
cob, if necessary, and mix with ground beef. Put the yogurt and
the egg in the blender. Purée well. Add this and all of the other
ingredients to the casserole dish, blending well. Sprinkle fresh
parsley over the top as a garnish. Bake for 50 minutes at 350° F. or
microwave on high for 20 minutes. This casserole is done when the
center is firm and the top is lightly browned. This may be
assembled, frozen and thawed for later baking.

Calories per 3/4 c. serving: 187
Fat: 5 gm. Cholesterol: 40 mg. with egg, 8 mg. with substitute
Sodium: 172 mg. with salt, 109 mg. without
For exchange diets, count:
2 lean meat, 1 bread/starch.

"Hands on" preparation time: 15 min.
Baking time: conventional oven, 50 min.; microwave oven, 20 min.

Time Saver Lasagne
Yield: 4 servings

* * *

This is a quick meatless version of the family favorite.

---

9 lasagne noodles
8 oz. can tomato sauce
1/2 tsp. basil
1/2 tsp. thyme
1/4 tsp. black pepper
1 1/2 c. part-skim ricotta
    cheese
1 clove garlic, minced
1 egg
4 oz. part-skim mozzarella
    cheese, shredded
1 oz. part-skim cheddar
    cheese, shredded

Cook noodles according to package directions. Combine tomato sauce, basil, thyme and pepper in small saucepan. Bring to a boil and cook 1 minute. Combine ricotta, garlic and egg in small bowl. Combine shredded cheeses on wax paper. Preheat oven to 400° F. Spoon a thin layer of tomato sauce on the bottom of 9-inch by 9-inch baking dish. Arrange 3 cooked noodles on the sauce. Spread ricotta filling down length of strips. Layer noodles and ricotta mixture two more times, then cover pan with aluminum foil. Bake for 15 minutes. Reheat sauce and spoon over pasta. Cover with shredded cheeses. Bake uncovered for 10 more minutes. Cut and serve.

Calories per serving: 351
Fat: 15 gm. Cholesterol: 31 mg.
Sodium: 296 mg.
For exchange diets, count:
3 lean meat, 2 bread/starch, 1 vegetable

"Hands on" preparation time: 20 min.
Baking time: 25 min.

VEGETABLES

Barbecued Baked Potatoes
Yield: 4 servings, 1 cup each

* * *

2 slices bacon
1 TB. flour
1/4 tsp. salt
1/4 tsp. pepper
4 c. thinly sliced raw potatoes
1/2 c. chopped onion
2 oz. reduced-fat American cheese, shredded and then divided in half
1/4 c. ketchup
1 tsp. Worcestershire sauce
3 drops hot pepper sauce
1 1/2 c. skim milk

Dice bacon and place on a microwave broiling tray. Cover with a paper towel and cook on high power for 2 minutes. Drain well. In a small bowl, mix flour, salt and pepper. In a 2-quart microwave casserole dish, layer flour, potatoes, onions and half of cheese. Combine last four ingredients and pour over potatoes. Bake at 375° F. for 50 minutes. Stir gently, sprinkle with remaining cheese and bacon, and bake 5 more minutes. To microwave, cook on high power for 25 minutes. Stir, gently, and sprinkle with cheese and bacon. Cook at 50% power for 5 more minutes.

Calories per serving: 204
Fat: 4 gm. Cholesterol: 12 mg.
Sodium: 457 mg.
For exchange diets, count:
2 bread/starch, 1 fat
Nutrient Alert: To reduce sodium, omit salt.

"Hands on" preparation time: 10 min.
Baking time: conventional oven, 55 min.; microwave oven, 30 min.

Brocciflower with Cheddar and Dill
Yield: 4 servings, 1 cup each

* * *

> 1 head fresh brocciflower
> (a pretty green vegetable that
> is a cross between broccoli
> and cauliflower)
> 1 oz. shredded part-skim
> cheddar cheese (such as
> Kraft Light and Natural®)
> 1 TB. dill seed

Wash brocciflower, remove woody stem and place in a microwave dish. Add 2 TB. water, cover, and cook on high power for 4 minutes. Remove from oven, and drain liquid. Sprinkle with shredded cheese and dill seed. Replace cover and allow cheese to melt, about 2 minutes. Cut into 4 portions and serve.

Calories per serving: 50
Fat: 1 gm. Cholesterol: 7 mg.
Sodium: 44 mg.
For exchange diets, count:
2 vegetable

"Hands on" preparation time: 10 min.

Brussels Sprouts Polonaise
Yield: 4 servings, 1 cup each

* * *

With this recipe from my friend Jane Siebrecht, everyone will enjoy your introduction to these little European cabbages.

---

1 lb. fresh Brussels sprouts
1/4 c. dry white wine such as chablis, sauterne, chardonnay or dry table wine
1 egg, hard boiled
1/4 c. fresh parsley, chopped fine (this is a must)
1 TB. margarine, melted
2 TB. lemon juice

First, boil the egg for 10 min. until hard; then chop fine. Meanwhile, wash sprouts and remove any brown spots. Place sprouts in a microwave-safe dish. Sprinkle with wine, cover and cook on high power for 5 minutes. In a small cup, mix parsley, margarine and lemon juice. Microwave on high power for 20 seconds, until margarine is melted. Remove cover from sprouts, drain if necessary, and sprinkle with chopped egg and parsley mixture. Serve.

Calories per serving: 85
Fat: 4 gm. Cholesterol: 68 mg.
Sodium: 68 mg.
For exchange diets, count:
2 vegetable, 1 fat
Nutrient Alert: To reduce cholesterol, use white of egg only.

"Hands on" preparation time: 15 min.

FIVE BEAN SIDE DISH
YIELD: 8 SERVINGS, 1 1/2 CUPS EACH

* * *

---

8 slices bacon, broiled and
   crumbled
1/3 c. sugar
2 TB. cornstarch
3/4 c. vinegar
1/2 c. water
16 oz. can no-added-salt green
   beans
16 oz. can lima beans
16 oz. can wax beans
15 oz. can kidney beans
15 oz. can garbanzo beans

Combine sugar, cornstarch, vinegar, and water with whisk in a
medium-sized skillet. Cook and stir to boiling. Drain all the
beans well. Add the beans to the skillet, just stirring to mix.
Simmer for 20 minutes. Meanwhile, broil and crumble bacon.
Stir bacon into beans and serve. This casserole can be prepared
and frozen for later use.

Calories per serving: 255
Fat: 4 gm. Cholesterol: 6 mg.
Sodium: 411 mg.
For exchange diets, count:
1 1/2 bread/starch, 1 vegetable, 2 lean meat.

"Hands on" preparation time: 10 min.
Cooking time: 20 min.

Good Fortune Chinese Vegetables
Yield: 4 servings, 1 cup each

* * *

> 2 cups raw veggies for stir-fry
> I like this combo:
> > 1/2 c. pea pods
> > 1/2 c. broccoli
> > 1/4 c. green pepper
> > 1/4 c. mushrooms
> > 1/4 c. water chestnuts
> > 1/4 c. carrots
>
> 1 TB. oil
> 1/2 c. tofu
> 1 c. quick rice
> 1 c. water
> 1 tsp. soy sauce
> 1/2 tsp. sugar
> 1/8 tsp. white pepper
> 2 TB. cornstarch
> 1 tsp. oyster sauce

Slice all vegetables into bite-size pieces. Pre-heat oil in wok or large skillet for 2 minutes. Add all vegetables and tofu. Stir-fry for 1 minute, then cover for 4 minutes. Meanwhile, combine rice and 1 cup of water in covered microwave dish. Cook on high power for 3 minutes. Add soy sauce, sugar, and pepper to vegetables. Mix well. Blend cornstarch with oyster sauce in a small bowl and add to vegetable mixture, tossing until mixture is smooth. Serve vegetables at once over rice.

Calories per serving: 196
Fat: 6 gm. Cholesterol: 0 mg.
Sodium: 185 mg.
For exchange diets, count:
3 vegetable, 1 fat, 1 bread/starch

"Hands on" preparation time: 15 min.

ITALIAN VEGETABLE MEDLEY
YIELD: 4 SERVINGS, 1 CUP EACH

* * *

2 medium zucchini, sliced
2 yellow squash, sliced
2 medium tomatoes, peeled
  and chopped
1 TB. margarine, melted
1/4 tsp. salt
1/4 tsp. garlic powder or
  1 clove garlic, minced
1/2 tsp. basil
2 TB. Parmesan cheese

Combine zucchini, yellow squash and tomatoes in a microwave dish. Sprinkle mixture with melted margarine, salt, garlic, basil and cheese. Cover and microwave on high power for 7 minutes, until vegetables are tender crisp. Serve.

Calories per serving: 71
Fat: 4 gm. Cholesterol: 2 mg.
Sodium: 221 mg.
For exchange diets, count:
1 vegetable, 1 fat

"Hands on" preparation time: 15 min.

Orange Glazed Sugar Snap Peas
Yield: 4 servings, 1 cup each

* * *

---

1 lb. sugar snap peas, fresh or
   frozen
1 TB. brown sugar
2 TB. orange juice
   concentrate, thawed
1 TB. margarine

Place peas with 1 TB. water in a microwave dish. Cover and cook
on high power for 4 minutes. Remove from oven, and drain
liquid. Combine brown sugar, orange juice concentrate, and
margarine in a small cup. Microwave on high power for 30
seconds. Drizzle over peas and serve.

Calories per serving: 89
Fat: 1 gm. Cholesterol: 0 mg.
Sodium: 16 mg.
For exchange diets, count:
2 vegetable, 1/2 fruit

"Hands on" preparation time: 10 min.

Picnic Green Beans
Yield: 4 servings, 2 cups each

* * *

> 2 lb. fresh green beans or
> 2 (1 lb.) cans of no-added-
> salt green beans, drained
>
> 2 strips bacon, diced
>
> 8 oz. can mushroom pieces,
> drained
>
> 1 TB. grated onion
>
> 1 c. reduced-sodium canned
> tomato soup, undiluted
> (such as Campbell's
> Healthy Request®)
>
> 2 TB. brown sugar
>
> 2 tsp. prepared mustard

Steam beans until nearly tender, about 6 minutes. Microwave diced bacon on a broiling tray for 2 minutes and drain well. In a 3-quart casserole dish, combine bacon, mushrooms, onion, tomato soup, brown sugar and mustard. Mix well. Gently stir in steamed or canned green beans. Bake for 20 minutes at 350° F., or microwave uncovered on 50% power for 8 minutes.

Calories per serving: 157
Fat: 3 gm. Cholesterol: 2 mg.
Sodium: 311 mg.
For exchange diets, count:
3 vegetable, 1 fat, 1/2 bread/starch

"Hands on" preparation time: 10 min.
Cooking time: conventional oven, 20 min.; microwave oven, 8 min.

Sandy's Red Beans and Rice
Yield: 8 servings, 2 cups each

An unforgettable dish prepared for our gourmet club by Sandy Sieg.

> 1 lb. red beans, washed
> thoroughly and drained
> 1 clove garlic, minced
> 3 c. red wine
> 1 c. water
> 1 TB. Worcestershire sauce
> 2 tsp. Louisiana hot sauce
> 2 slices bacon, diced
> 2 medium onions, chopped
> 6 cups cooked rice

Marinate beans in wine, water, garlic, Worcestershire sauce and hot sauce overnight. The next day, cook bacon until crisp in heavy stockpot. Drain bacon grease. Add onions and the bean mixture to the stockpot. Cook beans on high for 6 hours in the crockpot, or for 1 1/2 hours on medium heat on the stove top, or for 30 minutes in a pressure cooker at 15 lb. of pressure. If beans begin to appear dry during cooking, add 1/2 c. water. When beans are done to desired tenderness, add salt and serve over cooked rice.

Calories per serving: 319
Fat: 2 gm. Cholesterol: 2 mg.
Sodium: 46 mg.
For exchange diets, count:
3 bread/starch, 1 lean meat, 1 vegetable

"Hands on" preparation time: 10 min.
Cooking time: crockpot, 6 hr.; stove top, 1 1/2 hr.;
pressure cooker, 30 min.

Shredded Zucchini and Yellow Squash in a Skillet
Yield: 4 servings, 1 cup each

* * *

3 zucchini
3 yellow squash
1 TB. margarine
1/4 tsp. salt
1/4 tsp. freshly ground pepper
1 TB. fresh chives, chopped
   fine

Peel zucchini and summer squash. Shred over coarse side of grater or in food processor. In large skillet, melt margarine over high heat. Add shredded squash and cook for 5 minutes. Season with salt, pepper, and chives just before serving.

Calories per serving: 47
Fat: 3 gm. Cholesterol: 0 mg.
Sodium: 169 mg.
For exchange diets, count:
1 vegetable, 1/2 fat

"Hands on" preparation time: 10 min.
Cooking time: 5 min.

STIR-FRIED BROCCOLI AND CARROTS
YIELD: 4 SERVINGS, 1 CUP EACH

* * *

1 tsp. vegetable oil
2 thin slices ginger root or 1/2
   tsp. ginger
1 clove garlic, minced
1 1/2 c. chopped fresh broccoli
1 c. thinly sliced carrots
1 small onion, sliced into
   rings
3/4 c. no-added-salt chicken
   broth
1 TB. cornstarch
1 TB. cold water
1 c. sliced mushrooms
2 TB. oyster sauce (may
   substitute reduced-sodium
   soy sauce)

Heat oil in wok or large no-stick skillet until hot. Add ginger and garlic and stir 1 minute. Add broccoli, carrots and onion and stir-fry 1 minute. Add chicken broth. Cover and cook 3 minutes. Meanwhile, mix cornstarch with water and stir into mixture. Stir mixture until thickened, then add mushrooms and oyster sauce. Cook 1 more minute, transfer to a platter and serve.

Calories per serving: 78
Fat: 2 gm. Cholesterol: 0 mg.
Sodium: 306 mg.
For exchange diets, count:
3 vegetable

"Hands on" preparation time: 15 min.

Tangy Green Beans
Yield: 4 servings, 2 cups each

* * *

Thanks, Kay Wolf!

> 2 lb. fresh green beans,
>   washed, stemmed and cut
>   into 1-in. pieces
> 1 TB. margarine
> 2 TB. sugar
> 2 TB. Dijon mustard
> 2 TB. vinegar
> 2 TB. lemon juice

Using a steamer, steam beans until tender, 6 to 8 minutes.
Meanwhile, place margarine in a microwave-safe serving bowl.
Microwave margarine on high until melted, about 20 seconds.
Stir in remaining ingredients. Transfer drained beans to the
serving bowl, toss with margarine and seasonings. Serve.

Calories per serving: 120
Fat: 4 gm. Cholesterol: 0 mg.
Sodium: 133 mg.
For exchange diets, count:
1 fat, 1 vegetable

"Hands on" preparation time: 15 min.

Tipsy Sweet Potatoes
Yield: 4 servings, 1 potato each

* * *

Kay Vifian found this trick for making sweet potatoes irresistible.

> 4 large sweet potatoes
> 1 TB. margarine
> 2 TB. skim milk
> 2 TB. honey
> 1 tsp. rum flavoring
> 1/2 tsp. cardamom
> 1/4 tsp. salt
> 2 TB. walnuts

Preheat oven to 400° F. Wash potatoes. Place in a microwave dish with 2 TB. water. Cover and cook on high power for 15 minutes. Cool under cold water. Cut off top third of potato and discard. Use a spoon to remove majority of pulp from shell. Place pulp in a mixing bowl. Add margarine, milk, honey, rum flavoring, cardamom and salt to pulp. Beat smooth. Stuff pulp back into potato shells. Sprinkle top with walnuts. Bake at 400° F. for 10 minutes.

Calories per serving: 260
Fat: 7 gm. Cholesterol: less than 1 mg.
Sodium: 186 mg.
For exchange diets, count:
3 bread/starch, 1/2 fat

"Hands on" preparation time: 25 min.

VEGETABLE STUFFING
YIELD: 8 SERVINGS, 1 CUP EACH

* * *

> 1 TB. margarine
> 1 pkg. herbed stuffing mix
> 2 c. zucchini, broccoli or
>   cabbage, cut into bite-sized
>   pieces
> 1 medium onion, chopped
> 3 carrots, finely shredded
> 1 c. no-added-salt chicken
>   broth

Measure margarine into a 3-quart microwave-safe casserole dish.
Microwave on high power for 20 seconds. Open herbed stuffing
mix. Reserve 1 cup stuffing. Combine remaining stuffing mix
and all other ingredients with the melted margarine. Pat evenly
into the casserole dish. Sprinkle reserved bread cubes on top.
Bake in oven at 350° F., for 45 minutes; or microwave on high
power for 20 minutes, turning twice during cooking.

Calories per serving: 230
Fat: 4 gm. Cholesterol: 0 mg.
Sodium: 410 mg.
For exchange diets, count:
1 vegetable, 2 bread/starch, 1 fat

"Hands on" preparation time: 10 min.
Baking time: conventional oven, 45 min.; microwave oven, 20 min.

You'll Love Chutney
Yield: 4 servings, 3/4 cup each

* * *

A wonderful side dish for poultry.

1/4 c. sugar
1/4 c. cider vinegar
1 tsp. ginger
1/4 tsp. cumin
1/8 tsp. salt
1/2 c. chopped onion
1/3 c. dried apricots, each
   quartered
1/4 c. raisins
1 c. pineapple tidbits, drained

In a 2-quart saucepan, combine the first five ingredients. Bring to a boil over high heat, and then stir in onions, apricots, and raisins. Reheat to boiling, and then reduce heat to simmer for 5 minutes. Cool slightly and stir in pineapple. Refrigerate for 30 minutes and serve.

Calories per serving: 156
Fat: less than 1 gm. Cholesterol: 0 mg.
Sodium: 70 mg.
For exchange diets, count:
2 fruit, 1 vegetable

"Hands on" preparation time: 15 min.
Chilling time: 30 min.

Zucchini with Almonds
Yield: 4 servings, 1 cup each

* * *

1/2 c. chopped onion
1 TB. water
1/4 tsp. salt
4 c. sliced zucchini or yellow
squash or carrots or a
mixture
2 TB. sliced almonds
1 tsp. margarine
1/2 tsp. marjoram
1/2 tsp. lemon juice
1/8 tsp. white pepper
1 TB. grated Parmesan
cheese.

In a 3-quart microwave casserole dish, combine onion, water and salt. Cover and microwave on high power for 2 minutes. Stir in zucchini. Cover and cook on high power for 5 minutes. Drain. In a skillet, melt margarine and sauté almonds until browned. Sprinkle over drained vegetables. Sprinkle with marjoram, lemon juice and pepper. Toss gently. Cover and microwave on high power for 1 minute. Sprinkle with Parmesan cheese and serve.

Calories per serving: 72 cal.
Fat: 5 gm. Cholesterol: 1 mg.
Sodium: 171 mg.
For exchange diets, count:
1 vegetable, 1 fat

"Hands on" preparation time: 15 min.

MEATS, POULTRY AND FISH

Beef Burgundy in a French Bread Crust
Yield: 4 servings, 3 oz. each

* * *

1 lb. frozen bread dough, thawed

1 egg white plus 2 TB. water mixed together

1 lb. beef stew meat, well trimmed

10 oz. beef broth (may use no-added-salt beef broth)

3/4 c. burgundy wine

1 medium onion, sliced thin

1/4 c. bread crumbs

1/4 c. flour

1/4 tsp. salt

1/4 tsp. pepper

8 oz. fresh mushrooms, sliced thin

Form thawed bread dough into four small round loaves. Place them on a baking sheet that has been sprayed with nonstick cooking spray. Cover and put in a warm place, allowing to rise until double in bulk, about 1 hour. Preheat oven to 425° F. Brush tops of loaves with egg white and water. Bake for 15 minutes, until browned. Meanwhile, in a small mixing bowl, combine flour and bread crumbs and set aside. Slice mushrooms and onion and place them either in a crockpot or in a 2-quart casserole dish. Add meat, wine, broth, salt and pepper to crockpot or casserole dish. Blend. Stir flour and bread crumb mixture into meat and cover. Cook meat in crockpot for 6 hours on high, or in conventional oven at 300° F. for 3 hours, until mixture is thick. When mixture is done, use a sharp knife to cut out the inside of bread loaves, leaving a 1 1/2 - inch crust. Serve meat in the bread crust. Eat scooped out bread on the side.

Calories per serving: 391
Fat: 6 gm. Cholesterol: 72 mg.
Sodium: 542 mg.
For exchange diets, count:
2 bread/starch, 4 lean meat
(Nutrient analysis includes 1/4 of the loaf of bread in each serving.)

"Hands on" preparation time: 15 min.
Bread rising and baking time: 1 hr. 15 min.
Meat cooking time: crockpot, 6 hours; conventional oven, 3 hours

BEER-GRILLED SIRLOIN
YIELD: 4 SERVINGS

* * *

1 lb. sirloin, well trimmed and
portioned into 4 steaks

Marinade:
1/4 c. reduced-sodium soy
sauce
1 c. beer
2 TB. brown sugar
1 tsp. ground ginger

Combine marinade ingredients in a shallow bowl or pan. Add
sirloin. Cover and refrigerate for at least 30 minutes, or up to 24
hours. Grill over medium-hot flame for 4 minutes per side,
turning once.

Calories per serving: 213
Fat: 6 gm. Cholesterol: 69 mg.
Sodium: 547 mg.
For exchange diets, count:
4 lean meat

"Hands on" preparation time: 5 min.
Chilling time: 30 min.
Grilling time: 8 min.

BROILED HAM WITH ORANGE GLAZE
YIELD: 4 SERVINGS, 4 OZ. EACH

* * *

1/4 c. frozen orange juice
  concentrate, thawed
1 TB. brown sugar
1 TB. cider vinegar
3/4 tsp. dry mustard
1/4 tsp. ginger
1 lb. lean ham, cut into 4
  slices

In small bowl, combine first five ingredients. Place ham slices on broiler pan. Broil under low flame, 3 minutes on each side, stopping to baste meat with glaze several times during cooking.

Calories per serving: 196
Fat: 6 gm. Cholesterol: 48 mg.
Sodium: 1,179 mg.
For exchange diets, count:
3 lean meat, 1/2 fruit
Nutrient Alert: To reduce sodium, substitute fresh lean pork for ham.

"Hands on" preparation time: 5 min.
Broiling time: 6 min.

Chicken and Noodles with Red Sauce
Yield: 4 servings

* * *

> 1 medium onion, sliced
> 2 cloves garlic, minced
> 1 tsp. rosemary
> 1/2 tsp. basil
> 1/2 tsp. thyme
> 1 TB. vegetable oil
> 16 oz. can chunky tomatoes,
>   drained
> 3/4 c. ketchup
> 1/4 c. cider vinegar
> 1 TB. brown sugar
> 1/4 tsp. salt
> Dash pepper
> 4 chicken breasts, skinned
> Hot cooked noodles or rice

In Dutch oven or large skillet, sauté onion, garlic and herbs in oil, until onion is tender-crisp. Stir in tomatoes and next 5 ingredients. Add chicken breasts. Bring to a boil. Reduce the heat and simmer, covered, for 20 minutes. Meanwhile, prepare noodles. Serve chicken in red sauce over noodles or rice.

Calories per serving: 238
Fat: 6 gm. Cholesterol: 69 mg.
Sodium: 806 mg.
For exchange diets, count:
4 lean meat, 1 vegetable
(Analysis does not include noodles or rice.)
Nutrient Alert: To reduce sodium, use reduced-sodium ketchup and omit salt.

"Hands on" preparation time: 10 min.
Cooking time: 20 min.

Chicken Teriyaki with Pineapple
Yield: 4 servings

* * *

2 chicken breasts, cut in
    half, skinned, and
    deboned
1 small onion, chopped
1 clove garlic, minced
1 tsp. vegetable oil
1/4 tsp. salt
2 TB. orange juice stirred
    with 2 tsp. cornstarch
2 TB. dry sherry

1 TB. soy sauce
1 tsp. dry mustard
1/4 tsp. ground ginger
8 oz. can pineapple
    chunks in juice,
    drained
1 green pepper, cut
    into 1-in. pieces

Garnish:
2 TB. sliced almonds

Pound skinned and deboned chicken breast halves between
sheets of wax paper to 1/4 inch thickness. Set aside. In a 2-quart
microwave casserole dish, combine all remaining ingredients
except almonds. Cover and cook on high power for 2 minutes. If
using a stove, cook pineapple mixture over medium heat for 5
minutes, stirring constantly until thick. Arrange chicken breast
halves on top of pineapple mixture, with thickest part of breast
toward the outside. Cover and microwave on high power for 8
minutes, turning chicken and rearranging after 4 minutes. Let
stand for 2 minutes. Garnish with almonds and serve. If using a
conventional oven, bake at 375° for 35 to 40 minutes.

Calories per serving: 263
Fat: 10 gm. Cholesterol: 69 mg.
Sodium: 504 mg.
For exchange diets, count:
3 lean meat, 1 fruit, 1 vegetable

"Hands on" preparation time: 10 min.
Cooking time: 10 min.

Cornflake Chicken or Fish
Yield: 4 servings, 3 oz. each

* * *

> 2 egg whites, whipped
> 1 1/2 c. evaporated skim milk
> 1 tsp. poultry seasoning
> 3 c. crushed cornflakes
> 1 lb. chicken, skinned, in
> pieces or 1 lb. frozen fish
> fillets

Preheat oven to 400° F. Combine egg whites, milk and seasoning in a mixing bowl. Whip for 2 minutes. Meanwhile, crush cornflakes in a plastic bag. Dip chicken or fish in milk and egg mixture, then shake in bag with cornflakes and place on a baking sheet. For chicken, bake at 400° F. for 35 to 45 minutes. For fish, reduce time to 15 to 20 minutes.

Calories per 3 oz. serving: 215
Fat: 9 gm. Cholesterol: 66 mg.
Sodium: 230 mg.
For exchange diets, count:
3 lean meat, 1/2 bread/starch.

"Hands on" preparation time: 10 min.
Baking time: chicken, 45 min.; fish, 20 min.

CROCKPOT BEEF ROAST WITH FAT-FREE GRAVY
YIELD: 8 SERVINGS, 3 OZ. EACH

* * *

---

2 lb. chuck roast, well
   trimmed

12 oz. beer

.75 oz. (or 1/2 package) dry
   vegetable soup mix

2 TB. ketchup

2 TB. cold water

1 1/2 TB. cornstarch

Pour beer, soup mix and ketchup into the crockpot and stir well.
Place well-trimmed beef roast in the crockpot and cover. Cook on
low heat for 5 to 9 hours, or until desired tenderness. When the
meat is done, combine cornstarch and cold water in a small bowl.
Pour meat drippings from crockpot into a broth separator.
Slowly pour bottom portion (fat-free juice) into the cornstarch and
water. Whisk until smooth. Microwave for 1 minute on high
power; stir, and then microwave for 2 minutes on high power,
until gravy is thick. Serve gravy over meat and boiled or mashed
potatoes.

Calories per serving: 226
Fat: 8 gm. Cholesterol: 85 mg.
Sodium: 419 mg.
For exchange diets, count:
4 lean meat
Nutrient Alert: To reduce sodium, use no-added-salt soup mix.

"Hands on" preparation time: 10 min.
Crockpot time: 5 to 9 hr.

Crusty Fish with Herbs
in the Microwave
Yield: 4 servings

* * *

2 TB. lemon juice
2 TB. margarine
1 lb. fresh or thawed fish
   fillets, drained and patted
   dry
1 clove garlic, minced
1/2 c. bread crumbs
1/2 tsp. dried leaf basil
1/2 tsp. oregano
1 tsp. dried parsley, or 2 tsp.
   minced fresh parsley

Place fillets in a single layer in a 12-inch by 8-inch microwave baking dish. Sprinkle with lemon juice. Microwave margarine in a small custard cup on high power for 30 seconds, or until melted. Add remaining ingredients to cup and mix with a fork. Spoon bread crumb mixture over fish. Cover dish with paper towel. Microwave on high power for 8 minutes, or until fish flakes easily with a fork, turning twice during cooking. Remove paper towel and place dish under the broiler for 2 minutes to brown the crumbs. If using a conventional oven, bake at 425° F. for 20 minutes.

Calories per serving: 176
Fat: 7 gm. Cholesterol: 71 mg.
Sodium: 238 mg.
For exchange diets, count:
3 lean meat, 1 vegetable

"Hands on" preparation time: 10 min.
Cooking time: 10 min.

Fajita Pita
YIELD: 4 SERVINGS

* * *

4 pita pockets
1 lb. boneless chicken, cut
  into strips
1 green or red pepper, seeded
  and cut into thin strips
1 tsp. vegetable oil
1 tsp. lime juice
Picante sauce as desired

In a medium no-stick skillet, heat oil. Add lime juice and
chicken. Stir-fry until chicken is tender, about 8 minutes. Add
pepper strips. Continue cooking for 3 minutes. Stuff chicken and
peppers into pita pockets. Dot filling with picante sauce.

Calories per serving: 263
Fat: 5 gm. Cholesterol: 69 mg.
Sodium: 376 mg.
For exchange diets, count:
3 lean meat, 1 bread/starch, 1 vegetable

"Hands on" preparation time: 15 min.

Fajitas with Iowa Beef
Yield: 4 servings

* * *

This recipe is courtesy of my friends at the Iowa Beef Industry Council.

1/2 lb. beef top round steak or
  sirloin steak, cut 1/2 in. thick
2 1/2 TB. lime juice
1/4 tsp. garlic powder
1/4 tsp. black pepper
4 flour tortillas, warmed
1 c. shredded lettuce
1 c. chopped tomato
1 red or green pepper, cut into thin
  strips
1/4 c. chopped green onion
1/4 c. shredded part-skim
  mozzarella cheese
2 TB. plain lowfat yogurt

Pound meat to 1/4 inch thickness. Place in heavy plastic bag and
sprinkle with lime juice, garlic powder and pepper. Seal bag and
marinate for at least 30 minutes, or up to 24 hours in the refrigerator.
Remove meat from marinade and broil or panbroil for 3 minutes on
each side. Carve across the grain into thin slices. Meanwhile, put
tortillas on dinner plates and place lettuce, tomato, pepper, onion,
cheese and yogurt on each tortilla. Top with meat and serve.

Calories per serving: 276
Fat: 6 gm. Cholesterol: 40 mg.
Sodium: 374 mg.
For exchange diets, count:
1 bread/starch, 3 lean meat, 1 vegetable

"Hands on" preparation time: 20 min.
Marinating time: at least 30 min. or up to 24 hr.
Cooking time: 6 min.

Grilled Halibut with Pineapple Salsa

Yield: 4 servings, 4 oz. each

* * *

1 lb. halibut steaks, portioned into 4 servings	*Salsa:* 1 c. fresh pineapple, cut into fine chunks
Fish marinade:	1 small red bell pepper, diced
3 scallions, finely chopped	3 scallions, finely chopped
1/4 tsp. ginger	1 TB. jalapeno pepper, finely chopped
1 tsp. Dijon mustard	
1 tsp. dried cilantro or 2 TB. fresh cilantro leaves, minced	1/2 tsp. ginger
	1 TB. lime juice
	1TB. vinegar
1/4 c. lemon juice	1 tsp. sugar
1/4 c. water	1/8 tsp. salt

Combine ingredients for the marinade in a plastic bag. Place halibut steaks in bag and seal. Marinate 1/2 hour. Meanwhile, combine ingredients for salsa in a small serving bowl and refrigerate. Prepare grill. Remove halibut from marinade and grill over hot flame for 4 minutes per side, or until a fork can be inserted and removed from the flesh easily. Transfer to serving platter. Serve with salsa on the side.

Calories per serving: 190
Fat: 3 gm. Cholesterol: 71 mg.
Sodium: 183 mg.
For exchange diets, count:
3 lean meat, 1/2 fruit

"Hands on" preparation time: 15 min.
Marinating time: 30 min.
Grilling time: 20 min.

GRILLED TUNA STEAKS WITH SALSA
YIELD: 4 SERVINGS

* * *

1 lb. tuna steaks (or any firm
   white fish)
1/4 tsp. white pepper
1 clove garlic, minced
2 large ripe tomatoes, peeled,
   seeded and quartered
1 clove garlic, peeled
3 green onions, chopped
4 oz. can chopped green chilis
1 tsp. vegetable oil
1 TB. lime juice

Sprinkle tuna steaks with pepper and minced garlic. Use a fork
to work seasonings into the fish. Place steaks on a grilling rack
for fish or on a broiler pan. Grill for 10 minutes per inch of
thickness, turning once, until the fish flakes easily. To make
salsa, combine the tomatoes, garlic, onions, chilis, oil and lime
juice in a food processor or blender; process until coarsely
chopped. Turn tuna steaks onto a platter and top with salsa.
Serve at once.

Calories per serving: 131
Fat: 3 gm. Cholesterol: 71 mg.
Sodium: 118 mg.
For exchange diets, count:
2 lean meat, 1 vegetable

"Hands on" preparation time: 5 min.
Grilling time: 15 min.

Honey-Mustard Pork Chops
Yield: 4 servings

* * *

---

4 (3 oz.) pork chops, well
trimmed

Sauce:
4 TB. honey
2 TB. vinegar
2 TB. brown sugar
1 TB. Dijon-style mustard
1/2 tsp. paprika

Mix ingredients for sauce in a small bowl. Set aside. Grill chops over medium-hot flame for 8 minutes. Turn. Continue grilling for 4 minutes. Baste both sides with sauce. Grill for 4 more minutes, or until pork is cooked through.

Calories per serving: 244
Fat: 7 gm. Cholesterol: 63 mg.
Sodium: 85 mg.
For exchange diets, count:
3 lean meat, 1 1/2 fruit

"Hands on" preparation time: 20 min.

Hula Chicken with Rice
Yield: 4 servings, 3 oz. each

* * *

> 20 oz. can pineapple slices
>   packed in juice, undrained
> 2 skinless chicken breasts,
>   split
> 2 cloves garlic, minced
> 1/4 c. honey
> 2 TB. soy sauce
> 3 TB. cornstarch
> Grated peel from 1 lime
> 2 c. quick rice
> 2 c. water
> lime peel slivers for garnish

Rub chicken with garlic. Broil or grill chicken for 10 minutes, or until cooked through. While chicken is grilling, mix water and rice in 3-quart microwave dish. Cover and cook on high power for 5 minutes. Allow to sit 1 minute. While rice is cooking, drain pineapple juice into a 3-quart microwave dish. Stir in honey, lime juice, soy sauce, cornstarch and grated lime peel. Cook on high power for 3 minutes, stopping at 1 and 2 minutes to whisk. Add pineapple slices to sauce and stir. Rice can be cooked on stove, according to package directions. To cook pineapple on stove, heat over medium flame 5 to 8 minutes, stirring constantly until thick. Transfer rice to serving platter. Top with grilled chicken and pineapple sauce. Garnish with slivers of lime peel.

Calories per serving: 392
Fat: 3 gm. Cholesterol: 69 mg.
Sodium: 336 mg.
For exchange diets, count:
3 lean meat, 2 bread/starch, 1 fruit

"Hands on" preparation time: 20 min.

ITALIAN CHICKEN AND CHEESE
YIELD: 4 SERVINGS

* * *

1 1/2 c. water
1 c. quick rice
14 oz. can chunky tomatoes (undrained)
2 oz. reduced fat American cheese, diced
1/4 c. chopped onion
1/2 tsp. basil
1/2 tsp. oregano
2 chicken breasts, skinned and split in half
1/4 c. Parmesan cheese
1/4 tsp. garlic powder

If using conventional oven, preheat to 375° F. Stir together water, rice, tomatoes, cheese, onions, basil and oregano into a 3-quart casserole dish. Top with chicken. Mix Parmesan cheese with garlic powder in a small cup. Sprinkle over the chicken. Bake for 45 minutes, or until chicken is tender. To microwave, cook on 70% power for 15 to18 minutes, turning twice during cooking.

Calories per serving: 294
Fat: 6 gm. Cholesterol: 77 mg.
Sodium: 276 mg.
For exchange diets, count:
3 lean meat, 1 bread/starch, 2 vegetable

"Hands on" preparation time: 10 min.
Cooking time: conventional oven, 45 min.; microwave oven, 15 min.

Jambalaya
Yield: 8 servings, 1 1/2 c. each

* * *

> 2 TB. oil
> 1 large green pepper, diced
> 2 medium onions, chopped
> 1/2 tsp. garlic powder
> 1/2 c. cubed cooked lean ham
> 2 c. quick rice, uncooked
> 2 (1 lb., 12 oz.) cans no-added-salt tomatoes
> 1 tsp. hot pepper sauce
> 1 1/2 lb. peeled and deveined shrimp (For economy meal, may substitute chunks of white fish such as cod or haddock.)
> 1/2 tsp. pepper
> 1 tsp. basil
> 1/2 tsp. thyme

In 4-quart Dutch oven, heat oil. Sauté green pepper, onion and garlic. Add ham and brown. Stir in all remaining ingredients except for shrimp. Simmer for 20 minutes. Add shrimp or white fish and cook for 5 minutes, or until shrimp is pink, or white fish is tender and flaky. This dish can be prepared and frozen for later. Just thaw and reheat.

Calories per serving: 292
Fat: 5 gm. Cholesterol: 136 mg.
Sodium: 209 mg.
For exchange diets, count:
1 1/2 bread/starch, 2 vegetable and 2 lean meat.

"Hands on" preparation time: 15 min.
Cooking time: 25 min.

MICROWAVE MEATLOAF
YIELD: 4 SERVINGS, 4 OZ. EACH

* * *

1 egg or 1/4 c. liquid egg
  substitute
1/4 c. skim milk
1/4 c. oat bran or oatmeal
1/4 c. chopped onion
1/4 tsp. salt (optional)
1/2 tsp. pepper
1 lb. lean ground beef

Glaze:
1/4 c. no-added-salt tomato
  sauce
1 TB. brown sugar
1/2 tsp. prepared mustard
1/4 tsp. thyme

Combine ingredients for loaf in a 1-quart mixing bowl. Pat into
microwave-safe loaf pan. Cook, covered, for 14 minutes on high
power. Drain well. Combine ingredients for glaze. Spread over
the loaf. Cook on high power for 5 minutes. Let stand for 5 more
minutes, slice and serve. If using a conventional oven, bake at
375° F. for 40 minutes.

Calories per 4 oz. serving: 273
Fat: 12 gm. Cholesterol: 95 mg. with egg; 30 mg. with substitute
Sodium: 211 mg. with salt; 89 mg. with no salt
For exchange diets, count:
4 lean meat,1 bread/starch.

"Hands on" preparation time: 10 min.
Cooking time: 25 min.

Mom's Night Off
Submarine Sandwich
Yield: 4 servings

* * *

> 12-inch loaf French bread
> 4 oz. lean ham, sliced thin
> 4 oz. turkey, sliced thin
> 4 oz. part-skim Swiss cheese, sliced
> 1 tomato, sliced into 1/4-inch slices
> 4 large leaves lettuce
> 2 TB. mustard
> 2 TB. reduced-fat mayonnaise
> 2 tsp. honey

Split French bread lengthwise. Remove top half. On bottom half, layer ham, turkey, cheese, tomato and lettuce. In a small cup, mix together mustard, mayonnaise and honey. Spread on cut side of the top half. Place top half of bread on lettuce and slice into 4 servings, 3 inches each.

Calories per serving: 309
Fat: 8 gm. Cholesterol: 35 mg.
Sodium: 656 mg.
For exchange diets, count:
2 bread/starch, 3 lean meat
(To reduce sodium, substitute lean roast beef for ham.)

"Hands on" preparation time: 10 min.

No-Fat Fried Chicken
Yield: 4 servings

* * *

Enjoy a crispy piece of chicken with no added fat.

> 3 TB. grated Parmesan
> cheese
> 1/2 c. dry bread crumbs
> 1/2 tsp. rosemary
> 1/2 tsp. thyme
> 1/4 tsp. garlic powder
> 1/4 tsp. onion powder
> 1/4 tsp. black pepper
> 4 chicken breast halves,
> skinned, deboned and
> patted dry
> 3/4 c. buttermilk

Preheat oven to 400° F. Cover a baking sheet with foil and spray
with nonstick cooking spray. Combine all ingredients except
chicken and buttermilk in a shallow dish. Pour buttermilk into
another shallow dish. Dip chicken in the buttermilk, then roll in
dry mixture and set on baking sheet. Bake chicken for 35 to 40
minutes, until golden brown.

Calories per serving: 183
Fat: 3 gm. Cholesterol: 45 mg.
Sodium: 313 mg.
For exchange diets, count:
3 lean meat

"Hands on" preparation time: 15 min.
Baking time: 40 min.

NO ORDINARY STEAK SANDWICH
YIELD: 4 SANDWICHES

* * *

> 1 medium red onion, thinly sliced
> 1 small green pepper, seeded and diced
> 1/4 c. chili sauce
> 1 TB. Dijon or spicy brown mustard
> 1/2 tsp. Worcestershire sauce
> 4 whole wheat sandwich rolls
> 2 oz. part-skim Monterey Jack cheese, shredded
> 1/2 lb. lean roast beef, thinly sliced

In a 3-quart microwave dish, combine onion and pepper and cover with plastic wrap. Microwave on high power for 2 minutes. Add chili sauce, mustard and Worcestershire sauce. Stir until well blended. Cover and microwave on high power for 1 more minute. On bottom half of each roll, layer beef slices, shredded cheese and deviled onion mixture. Cover with top half of roll. Place sandwiches on serving plate, about 1 inch apart. Microwave on 50% power for 3 minutes or until heated through.

Calories per serving: 247
Fat: 7 gm. Cholesterol: 37 mg.
Sodium: 352 mg.
For exchange diets, count:
1 vegetable, 1 1/2 bread/starch, 2 lean meat

"Hands on" preparation time: 15 min.

Recipe suited only for microwave.

POUR PIZZA

YIELD: 8 SERVINGS

* * *

1 pkg. active dry yeast	3 1/2 c. flour
1 1/3 c. lukewarm water	Cornmeal to dust pan
1/3 c. dried instant potatoes	1 1/2 c. pizza sauce (I prefer Thick and Hearty Ragu®)
1 TB. brown sugar	2 c. sliced vegetable topping
1/2 tsp. salt	4 oz. mozzarella cheese, shredded
1 TB. oil	
1 egg or 1/4 c. liquid egg substitute	1/4 c. Parmesan cheese

Mix yeast and water together in a large mixing bowl. Add potatoes, brown sugar, salt, oil, and egg, mixing well after each addition. Use a dough hook to mix in flour; process until mixture is smooth. Spray a 15-inch by 8-inch baking pan with nonstick cooking spray and dust with cornmeal. Pour or scrape dough onto the pan and use a fork to spread dough over bottom and up the sides of the pan. Cover and put in a warm place for 15 minutes. Top with pizza sauce, toppings and cheeses . Bake for 20 to 25 minutes at 375° F, until crust is golden.

Calories per serving: 316
Fat: 6 gm. Cholesterol: 41 mg.
Sodium: 1816 mg.
For exchange diets, count:
2 1/2 bread/starch, 3 vegetable, 1 lean meat
Nutrient Alert: To reduce sodium, use no-added-salt tomato sauce as the topping.

"Hands on" preparation time: 30 minutes (includes rising)
Baking time: 20 to 25 minutes

RIO GRANDE STEW
YIELD: 4 SERVINGS, 2 CUPS EACH

* * *

1 lb. boneless beef stew meat, trimmed well	1 tsp. cumin
1 tsp. vegetable oil	1 bay leaf
1/2 c. water	1/4 tsp. salt
10 1/2 oz. can no-added-salt beef broth	1 large carrot, sliced thin
1/2 c. chopped onion	10 oz. pkg. frozen corn, thawed
1/2 c. chopped celery	2 c. fresh cabbage, sliced into small pieces
1 clove garlic, minced	
1 1/2 tsp. oregano	1/2 c. cold water
1 1/2 tsp. ground coriander	3 TB. cornstarch

In a large stockpot, brown the beef in the cooking oil. When meat is no longer pink, add water, broth, celery, onion, garlic, oregano, coriander, cumin, bay leaf and salt. Bring to a boil. Add carrots, cabbage and thawed corn. Cover and simmer for 20 minutes or until carrots are tender. In a small cup, combine water and cornstarch. Use a whisk and stir cornstarch into stew. Continue cooking for 3 minutes. Mixture will be thick and smooth. Ladle into individual bowls.

Calories per serving: 269
Fat: 6 gm. Cholesterol: 72 mg.
Sodium: 207 mg.
For exchange diets, count:
1 bread/starch, 1 vegetable, 3 lean meat

"Hands on" preparation time: 20 min.
Cooking time: 23 min.

Shrimp Creole
Yield: 4 servings, 2 cups each

* * *

2 strips bacon	1 TB. brown sugar
1 c. chopped onion	1 tsp. Worcestershire
1 clove garlic, minced	sauce
1/2 c. chopped green	1/2 tsp. soy sauce
pepper	1 bay leaf
2/3 c. finely diced celery	1/4 tsp. black pepper
1 1/2 c. chunky tomatoes	1 lb. fresh or frozen
4 oz. tomato paste	shrimp (defrost if
1/2 tsp. basil	using frozen)
1/4 tsp. salt	2 c. quick rice
1/4 tsp. cayenne pepper	2 c. water

Dice bacon and place on a microwave broiling tray. Cover with a paper towel and microwave on high power for 2 minutes. Drain well. Meanwhile, spray a Dutch oven with nonstick cooking spray. Sauté the onion, green pepper, celery and garlic for 4 minutes. Stir in tomatoes, tomato paste, basil, salt, cayenne pepper, brown sugar, Worcestershire sauce, soy sauce, bay leaf and pepper. Bring to a boil, then reduce heat and simmer for 10 minutes. Bring to a second boil, then stir in bacon and shrimp. Continue boiling for 3 minutes or until shrimp is no longer opaque. Meanwhile, combine quick rice with water in a 1-quart microwave dish. Cover and microwave on high power for 4 minutes. Spoon cooked rice onto a serving platter or individual plates. Top with shrimp and sauce.

Calories per serving: 300
Fat: 3 gm. Cholesterol: 45 mg.
Sodium: 271 mg.
For exchange diets, count:
2 bread/starch, 2 lean meat, 1 vegetable

"Hands on" preparation time: 25 min.

SPANISH PORK CHOPS WITH PEPPERS
YIELD: 4 SERVINGS, 3 OZ. EACH

* * *

> 2 cloves garlic, minced
> 1/4 tsp. salt
> 1/2 tsp. black pepper
> 1 tsp. vegetable oil
> 4 pork chops, 3 oz. each
> 2 red peppers, seeded and cut into 1/4 inch strips (may substitute a 4 oz. jar of pimentos, drained and cut)
> 1/2 c. dry white wine such as chablis, chardonnay, or dry table wine
> 1/2 c. no-added-salt chicken broth
> 1 tsp. finely shredded lemon rind

Trim chops and place in a flat pan. Sprinkle with minced garlic, salt and pepper. Use a spoon or fork to mash seasonings into meat. Cover and refrigerate for 30 minutes or up to overnight. Heat oil in large no-stick skillet. Add chops and brown on each side. Remove from skillet. Add red peppers and sauté for 5 minutes. Remove peppers from the skillet. Add wine and broth to the skillet and bring to a boil. Return peppers and chops to the skillet and reduce heat to simmer. Cook uncovered for 15 minutes. Transfer to a serving plate and sprinkle with lemon rind.

Calories per serving: 194
Fat: 10 gm. Cholesterol: 63 mg.
Sodium: 170 mg.
For exchange diets, count:
3 lean meat, 1 vegetable

"Hands on" preparation time: 10 min.
Marinating time: 30 min. or up to 24 hr.
Cooking time: 30 min.

Steak Picado
Yield: 4 servings

* * *

1 lb. sirloin, well trimmed
2 cloves garlic, minced
1/4 tsp. salt
3 c. chopped onion
3 c. chopped green pepper
3 tsp. cumin
1 tsp. black pepper
1 c. chopped fresh tomato

Cut sirloin into 1/2 inch cubes. In a large no-stick skillet, brown sirloin with garlic and salt for 4 minutes. Stir in all remaining ingredients. Cook uncovered over medium heat until liquid from tomato has evaporated, about 10 minutes. Serve over rice or barley.

Calories per serving: 252
Fat: 8 gm. Cholesterol: 65 mg.
Sodium: 198 mg.
For exchange diets, count:
3 lean meat, 3 vegetable

"Hands on" preparation time: 20 min.

Stromboli
Yield: 4 servings, 3 oz. each

* * *

> 1 lb. loaf of French bread, cut
> in half lengthwise
> 1/2 lb. lean ground beef
> 1 medium onion, sliced thin
> 4 oz. fresh mushrooms, sliced
> thin
> 2 cloves fresh garlic, minced
> or 1/2 tsp. minced garlic
> 1/4 tsp. black pepper
> 1 c. prepared spaghetti sauce
> (I prefer Thick and Hearty
> Ragu®)
> 2 oz. mozzarella cheese,
> shredded

In a Dutch oven, brown beef and drain well. In same Dutch oven, sauté onion, and mushroom with garlic and pepper. Stir in drained meat and spaghetti sauce. Heat until bubbly. Spread meat mixture over both halves of French bread and top with cheese. Broil 6 inches under low flame for 10 minutes. Slice and serve.

Calories per serving: 332
Fat: 10 gm. Cholesterol: 46 mg.
Sodium: 402 mg.
For exchange diets, count:
2 bread/starch, 2 vegetable, 2 lean meat
Nutrient Alert: To reduce sodium, substitute no-added-salt tomato sauce for prepared spaghetti sauce.

"Hands on" preparation time: 25 min.

Stuffed Sole
Yield: 4 servings, 4 oz. each

* * *

> 1 c. sliced mushrooms
> 1/2 c. sliced green onions
> 1 TB. vegetable oil
> 3/4 c. oatmeal or bread
>   crumbs
> 1 egg or 1/4 c. liquid egg
>   substitute
> 1/4 tsp. salt, optional
> 2 TB. lemon juice
> 1/2 tsp. marjoram
> 1 lb. sole, flounder, orange
>   roughy, or cod fillets
> Paprika

Preheat oven to 375° F. Sauté mushrooms and onions in oil for 3 minutes. Add oatmeal or bread crumbs, egg, salt, 1 TB. lemon juice and marjoram. Place stuffing mixture on top of fillets, spreading to within 1/2 inch of the edges. Roll up fillets and secure with toothpicks. Place seam side down in an 8-inch square baking dish. Sprinkle with the other 1 TB. of lemon juice, dust with paprika, and bake for 20 minutes. Or microwave for 8 minutes, just until the fish flakes easily with a fork.

Calories per serving: 260
Fat: 11 gm. Cholesterol: 114 mg. with egg, 50 mg. with substitute
Sodium: 263 mg. with salt, 141 mg. without salt
For exchange diets, count:
3 lean meat, 1 bread/starch.

"Hands on" preparation time: 15 min.
Baking time: conventional oven, 20 min.; microwave oven, 8 min.

TACO RICE DELIGHT
YIELD: 4 SERVINGS

* * *

1/2 lb. lean ground beef
1 medium onion, chopped
1/2 c. salsa
8 oz. can no-added-salt
tomato sauce
1 1/2 c. quick rice, uncooked
4 c. chopped lettuce
2 tomatoes, chopped
2 oz. part-skim cheddar
cheese, shredded

Brown ground beef and onion in a large skillet. Drain meat and return it to the skillet. Add salsa and tomato sauce to the meat and bring mixture to a boil. Stir in rice, cover and let stand for 5 minutes. Fluff rice with a fork, and transfer to a serving dish. Serve lettuce, tomatoes and cheese in side bowls as toppings.

Calories per serving: 342
Fat: 2 gm. Cholesterol: 50 mg.
Sodium: 198 mg.
For exchange diets, count:
2 bread/starch, 2 lean meat, 2 vegetable

"Hands on" preparation and cooking time: 15 min.

Tasty Marinade for Grilled White Fish
Yield: 3/4 c. or enough for 4 fillets

* * *

2 TB. vegetable oil
2 cloves garlic, minced
1 TB. fresh parsley or 1 tsp.
  dried parsley
1/2 c. orange juice
Juice of 1 fresh lemon or 2
  TB. bottled lemon juice
1 tsp. black pepper

Mix all ingredients in a shaker container and pour over your choice of white fish fillet. Cover and refrigerate for 30 minutes. Remove fish from marinade and grill over a hot flame for 10 min. per inch of thickness; or pan-grill in a no-stick skillet until fish flakes easily with a fork.

Calories per serving: 75
Fat: 6 gm. Cholesterol: 0 mg.
Sodium: less than 1 mg.
For exchange diets, count:
1/2 fruit, 1 fat
(Nutrient analysis does not include fish.)

"Hands on" preparation time: 5 min.
Marinating time: 30 min.
Cooking time: 15 min.

Veggie Meatloaf
YIELD: 4 SERVINGS, 4 OZ. EACH

* * *

1 lb. lean ground beef
1 carrot, grated
1 small onion, chopped
1 small stalk celery, diced
1 tsp. dried parsley or 2 tsp.
  minced fresh parsley
1 clove garlic, minced
1/8 tsp. nutmeg
1 tsp. Worcestershire sauce

Sauce:
1 c. no-added-salt tomato
  sauce
1/2 tsp. dry mustard
1/4 tsp. oregano
1/4 tsp. pepper
1 TB. brown sugar

Preheat oven to 375° F. Combine lean ground beef with
vegetables and seasonings. Pat into loaf pan. Mix ingredients for
sauce and pour over meat. Bake for 50 minutes. To microwave,
assemble loaf in microwave-safe loaf pan. Microwave on high
power for 14 min. Spread sauce over the loaf. Cook on high
power for 5 more minutes.

Calories per serving: 274
Fat: Cholesterol: 84 mg.
Sodium: 72 mg.
For exchange diets, count:
4 lean meat, 2 vegetables

"Hands on" preparation time: 10 min.
Baking time: conventional oven, 50 min.; microwave oven, 20 min.

White Fish with Picante Glaze
Yield: 4 servings

* * *

1 lb. frozen fish fillets,
  (suggest cod, orange
  roughy, or halibut)
1 c. picante sauce

Preheat oven to 425° F. Place fillets in a single layer in a 12-inch by 8-inch baking dish. Pour sauce over fish. Bake for 20 to 25 minutes, until fish flakes easily with a fork. Serve with a green salad and corn bread.

Calories per serving: 220
Fat: 4 gm. Cholesterol: 71 mg.
Sodium: 350 mg.
For exchange diets, count:
3 lean meat, 1 vegetable

"Hands on" preparation time: 10 min.
Cooking time: 20 min.

White Fish with Teriyaki Glaze
Yield: 4 servings

* * *

> 1 lb. frozen fish fillets,
> (suggest cod, orange
> roughy, or halibut)
> 1/4 c. reduced sodium
> terikyaki sauce
> 1 clove garlic, minced
> 1/4 tsp. black pepper

Preheat oven to 425° F. Place fillets in a single layer in a 12-inch by 8-inch baking dish. Pour sauce over fish. Sprinkle top with garlic and pepper. Bake for 20 to 25 minutes, until fish flakes easily with a fork. Serve with stir-fried vegetables and rice.

Calories per serving: 139
Fat: 4 gm. Cholesterol: 71 mg.
Sodium: 345 mg.
For exchange diets, count:
3 lean meat

"Hands on" preparation time: 10 min.
Cooking time: 20 min.

White Fish with Vegetables in the Microwave
Yield: 4 servings, 4 oz. each

* * *

1 carrot
3 small potatoes
1 leek or large onion
1 stalk celery
1 TB. margarine
1/4 tsp. salt
1/4 tsp. pepper
1/4 tsp. thyme
1 TB. cream sherry
1 lb. white fish fillets, no
 more than 1/2-inch thick,
 thawed

Spray microwave baking dish with nonstick cooking spray. Cut vegetables julienne-style and layer on bottom of dish. Dot with margarine. Sprinkle with salt, pepper, thyme and sherry. Add fish fillets. Cover and microwave on high power for 8 minutes, rotating dish every 2 minutes. If using a conventional oven, bake at 400° F. for 20 to 25 minutes.

Calories per serving: 259
Fat: 5 gm. Cholesterol: 71 mg.
Sodium: 302 mg.
For exchange diets, count:
1 bread/starch, 3 lean meat, 1 vegetable

"Hands on" preparation time: 10 min.
Cooking time: 8 min.

You Can Microwave Pork Roast
Yield: 8 servings, 3 oz. each

* * *

> 2 lb. boneless pork roast,
> trimmed well
> 1 c. reduced-calorie Italian
> dressing

Pour dressing over roast and rub into meat. Place meat on a microwave baking rack and cover well, but loosely, with microwave plastic wrap. Cook for 6 minutes at 90% power. Then reduce power to 40% and continue cooking to an internal temperature of 165° F. This will take from 20 to 25 minutes. Use a meat thermometer to check doneness. Remove from oven and wrap with aluminum foil. Roast will continue cooking, and the temperature will increase to 170° F. Slice and serve. If using a conventional oven, roast at 350° F. for 1 hour 15 minutes or until internal temperature reaches 165°.

Calories per serving: 243
Fat: 12 gm. Cholesterol: 83 mg.
Sodium: 301 mg.
For exchange diets, count:
4 lean meat

"Hands on" preparation time: 5 min.
Cooking time: 25 min.

DESSERTS

Better Than Sex Cake
Yield: 12 servings

* * *

> 1 pkg. 94% fat-free yellow
>   cake mix
> 20 oz. can crushed pineapple
>   in its own juice
> 1/4 c. sugar
> 2 pkg. instant vanilla
>   pudding mix
> 1 1/2 c. skim milk
> 3/4 c. flaked coconut, toasted

Prepare cake according to package directions in a 9-inch by 13-inch cake pan. Meanwhile, in a medium saucepan, combine pineapple with its juice and sugar. Cook over medium heat, stirring occasionally until thick, about 15 minutes. When cake is done, remove from oven and pierce top with a fork at 1 inch intervals. Pour on pineapple mixture and spread evenly. Cool cake completely. To speed cooling, place cake in the refrigerator. In medium bowl, combine pudding mix with milk, blending until thick. Spread over the pineapple. To toast coconut, place in flat plan and bake for 15 minutes in 350° oven. Sprinkle toasted coconut on top of frosted cake. Refrigerate until serving.

Calories per serving: 246
Fat: 3 gm. Cholesterol: 1 mg.
Sodium: 333 mg.
For exchange diets, count:
2 bread/starch, 1 fruit, 1/2 fat

"Hands on" preparation time: 20 min.
Baking time: 35 min.

Blueberry Crumble
Yield: 8 servings

* * *

3 c. fresh blueberries

1/4 c. frozen orange juice
concentrate, thawed

1 TB. sugar

1/2 c. oatmeal

1/4 c. whole wheat flour

2 TB. brown sugar

2 TB. margarine, cut into
small pieces

Preheat oven to 375° F. Combine first 3 ingredients in an 8-inch square baking dish. Set aside. Combine oats, flour and brown sugar in a bowl; cut in margarine with a pastry blender, until mixture resembles coarse meal. Sprinkle over berries. Bake for 30 minutes. Top with low-fat frozen yogurt.

Calories per serving: 110
Fat: 2 gm. Cholesterol: 0 mg.
Sodium: 21 mg.
For exchange diets, count:
1/2 bread/starch, 1 fruit

"Hands on" preparation time: 15 min.
Baking time: 30 min.

CARROT COOKIES
YIELD: 36

* * *

1/3 c. vegetable oil

3/4 c. sugar

1 c. cooked and mashed
carrots or 2 (4 oz.) jars
carrot baby food

3 eggs or 3/4 c. liquid egg
substitute

1 tsp. orange extract or 1 TB.
frozen orange juice
concentrate, thawed

2 1/4 c. flour

2 tsp. baking powder

1/2 tsp. salt

3/4 c. coconut

Preheat oven to 375° F. Cream vegetable oil, sugar and carrots
in a 3-quart mixing bowl. Beat in eggs, one at a time. Stir in
orange extract. In a separate small bowl, mix together last 4
ingredients. Add to carrot mixture and stir until well blended.
Drop by teaspoonfuls onto a no-stick cookie sheet. Bake for 10
minutes, or until firm.

Calories per serving: 80
Fat: 2 gm. Cholesterol: 23 mg. with egg, 0 mg. with substitute
Sodium: 85 mg.
For exchange diets, count:
1 bread/starch

"Hands on" preparation time: 15 min.
Baking time: 10 min.

CEREAL PIE CRUST
YIELD: FILLS ONE 9-INCH PIE PAN, OR 8 SERVINGS

* * *

> 1 1/2 c. crushed flaked dry
>   cereal
> 1/3 c. coconut
> 3 TB. brown sugar
> 2 TB. chopped nuts, such as
>   walnuts or almonds
> 1 TB. margarine, melted

Preheat oven to 350° F. Combine all ingredients in a large mixing bowl. Pour evenly into pie pan. Using wax paper, press firmly onto bottom and sides of pan. Bake for 9 minutes, or until lightly browned. Cool before filling.

Calories per serving: 88
Fat: 2 gm. Cholesterol: 0 mg.
Sodium: 151 mg.
For exchange diets, count:
1 bread/starch

"Hands on" preparation time: 20 min.

Chocolate Oatmeal Cookies
Yield: 24 cookies

* * *

2/3 c. flour
2/3 c. sugar
1 c. quick oatmeal
1/3 c. cocoa
1 tsp. baking powder
1/4 tsp. salt
2 egg whites
1/3 c. corn syrup
1 tsp. vanilla

Preheat oven to 350° F. Spray baking sheet with nonstick cooking spray. In a large mixing bowl, combine flour, sugar, oats, cocoa, baking powder and salt. Add egg whites, corn syrup and vanilla. Stir just until moist. Drop by spoonfuls onto cookie sheet. Bake for 10 minutes just until set. Cool for 5 minutes on the cookie sheet. Remove to wire rack.

Calories per serving: 70
Fat: 0 gm. Cholesterol: 0 mg.
Sodium: 90 mg.
For exchange diets, count: 1 fruit

"Hands on" preparation time: 15 min.
Baking and cooling time: 15 min.

Chocolate Cherry Cake
Yield: 12 servings

* * *

---

1 pkg. 94% fat-free chocolate
cake mix
20 oz. can cherry pie filling
2 eggs or 1/2 c. liquid egg
substitute
Powdered sugar

Preheat oven to 350° F. In a large mixing bowl, mix all
ingredients on low speed for 4 minutes, or until well blended.
Scrape bowl often. Bake for 35 minutes, or until inserted
toothpick comes back clean. Cool. Dust with powdered sugar.

Calories per serving: 236
Fat: 2 gm. Cholesterol: 45 mg. with egg, 0 mg. with substitute
Sodium: 303 mg.
For exchange diets, count:
2 bread/starch, 1 fat

"Hands on" preparation time: 10 min.
Baking time: 35 min.

Coconut Lover's Macaroons
Yield: 36 cookies

* * *

1/2 c. egg whites (separate 4
  large eggs)
1/4 tsp. salt
1 1/4 c. sugar
1 tsp. almond or vanilla
  extract
2 1/2 c. shredded coconut

Preheat oven to 325° F. With electric mixer, beat egg whites and
salt in a large mixing bowl, just until soft peaks form. Gradually
add sugar, beating until stiff peaks form. Fold in vanilla and
coconut. Drop batter from a spoon onto a baking sheet that has
been sprayed with nonstick cooking spray. Bake for 20 minutes.
Cool 10 minutes before removing from baking sheet.

Calories per serving: 53
Fat: 1 gm. Cholesterol: 0 mg.
Sodium: 33 mg.
For exchange diets, count:
1/2 bread/starch

"Hands on" preparation time: 15 min.
Baking and cooling time: 30 min.

Coffee-Flavored Chocolate Brownies
Yield: 24 brownies

* * *

19 oz. pkg. 94% fat-free
  brownie mix (such as Lovin'
  Lites® by Pillsbury)
1 beaten egg
1 TB. instant coffee dissolved
  in 1/3 c. hot water

Preheat the oven to 350° F. In large mixing bowl, combine egg, brownie mix and coffee dissolved in water. Mix by hand 75 strokes. Spread in a 13-inch by 9-inch pan that has been sprayed with nonstick cooking spray. Bake for 30 minutes. Brownies will appear soft; do not over-bake. Cool completely in pan on a wire rack. Cut into bars.

Calories per serving: 100
Fat: 2 gm. Cholesterol: 10 mg.
Sodium: 80 mg.
For exchange diets, count:
1 bread/starch, 1 fat

"Hands on" preparation time: 7 min.
Baking time: 30 min.

ENGLISH TRIFLE
YIELD: 12 SERVINGS

* * *

19 oz. pkg. 94% fat-free
   yellow cake mix
1 TB. dry sherry
3 1/2 oz. pkg. instant vanilla
   pudding or sugar free
   pudding mix
2 c. skim milk
2 c. strawberries or available
   fresh fruit, sliced

Prepare cake mix according to package directions, using a loaf
pan. Cool and slice into 12 slices. Cut each slice into 6 small
cubes. Meanwhile, combine pudding with milk, according to
package directions. In a 2-quart glass bowl, layer cake cubes;
sprinkle with 1 1/2 tsp. sherry, 1 cup fruit and 1 c. pudding.
Repeat. Garnish top with fresh berries. Chill at least 30 minutes
before serving.

Calories per serving: 191
Fat: 2 gm. Cholesterol: less than 1 mg.
Sodium: 311 mg.
For exchange diets, count:
2 bread/starch, 1/2 fruit

"Hands on" preparation time: 20 min.
Baking time: 35 min.
Chilling time: 30 min.

FRUITED PIE FILLING
YIELD: FILLS 1 PIE, OR 8 SERVINGS

* * *

2/3 c. sugar
1/2 c. water
1/4 c. cornstarch
3/4 c. cold water
1/8 tsp. salt
1 TB. lemon juice
1 TB. lemon, orange or
   strawberry gelatin dessert
   powder (may use sugar-free
   gelatin)
1 qt. prepared fresh fruit such
   as peaches, blueberries or
   strawberries

Combine sugar and water in a small saucepan. Bring to a boil.
In a small bowl, combine cornstarch, cold water, and salt. Slowly
stir into boiling sugar mixture. Cook 3 minutes or until thick.
Remove from heat and add lemon juice and gelatin dessert
powder. Cool. Meanwhile, prepare fruit and fill a prepared pie
crust. Pour cooled filling over fruit. Refrigerate 4 hours.

Calories per serving: 108
Fat: 0 gm. Cholesterol: 0 g.
Sodium: 35 mg.
For exchange diets, count:
1 1/2 fruit

"Hands on" preparation time: 20 min.
Chilling time: 4 hr.

Glazed Pineapple
Yield: 4 servings, 2 slices each

* * *

> 1 large pineapple
> 2 TB. sugar or equivalent in
>   sugar substitute
> 1/3 c. orange juice
> 3 TB. rum or 1 tsp. rum
>   extract
> 1 TB. honey

With sharp knife, cut off pineapple crown and stem end. Cut crosswise into 8 slices. Cut off peel, remove eyes and core. Sprinkle sugar into no-stick skillet. Add pineapple slices and sauté with sugar over medium heat for 5 minutes. Pour orange juice, rum and honey over pineapple and continue cooking for 3 minutes, until liquid begins to thicken. Remove slices to a serving platter and pour liquid over slices. Garnish with fresh mint.

Calories per serving: 124
Fat: less than 1 g. Cholesterol: 0 mg.
Sodium: 2 mg.
For exchange diets, count:
2 fruit

"Hands on" preparation time: 15 min.

Desserts

Lemon Angel Cake with Walnuts
Yield: 12 servings

* * *

> 1/3 c. chopped walnuts
> 1 pkg. angel food cake mix
> 1/2 c. frozen lemonade
>   concentrate, thawed
> 1 c. water
> 2 TB. grated lemon peel

Mix angel food cake mix according to package directions,
substituting lemonade concentrate and water for the water called
for in package directions. Fold lemon peel into prepared batter.
Spoon batter into 10-inch tube pan. Sprinkle with walnuts.
Bake and cool as directed. Top with bananas, peaches or
strawberries.

Calories per serving: 200
Fat: 2 gm. Cholesterol: 0 mg.
Sodium: 171 mg.
For exchange diets, count:
2 bread/starch, 1/2 fruit

"Hands on" preparation time: 10 min.
Baking time: 45 min.

MINT ANGEL CAKE
YIELD: 12 SERVINGS

* * *

1/4 c. chopped peppermint
   candies
1 pkg. angel food cake mix
1/3 c. frozen pink lemonade
   concentrate, thawed
1 1/3 c. cold water
chocolate ice milk (optional
   topping)

Preheat oven to 375° F. Place 8 hard peppermint candies in a
heavy plastic bag. Use a hammer to chop them fine. Prepare
cake mix according to package directions, substituting lemonade
concentrate for part of water. Fold in chopped peppermint
candy. Spoon batter into 10-inch tube pan. Top each serving
with 1/4 c. chocolate ice milk.

Calories per serving: 196
Fat: less than 1 g. Cholesterol: 0 mg.
Sodium: 174 mg.
For exchange diets, count:
2 bread/starch, 1/2 fruit

"Hands on" preparation time: 10 min.
Baking time: 40 min.

MISS PAT'S BREAD PUDDING
YIELD: 12 SERVINGS

* * *

```
4 eggs or 1 c. liquid egg
   substitute
1 1/2 c. sugar
1 TB. cinnamon
1 TB. nutmeg
1 TB. vanilla
2 TB. margarine, melted
3 c. skim milk
6 c. bread cubes
1/2 c. coconut
1/2 c. raisins

Glaze:
1/2 c. powdered sugar
1 tsp. rum extract
1 TB. skim milk
```

Preheat oven to 375° F. In a mixing bowl, beat first seven
ingredients until smooth. Spray an 11-inch x 7-inch baking dish
with nonstick cooking spray. Layer bread cubes, coconut, and
raisins into the dish. Pour egg and milk mixture over bread.
Bake for 40 minutes, or until set. Meanwhile, in a small cup, mix
together the ingredients for the glaze. Allow bread pudding to
cool slightly, then pour glaze over it, cut and serve.

Calories per serving: 220
Fat: 6 gm. Cholesterol: 92 mg. with eggs, 3 mg. with substitute
Sodium: 313 mg.
For exchange diets, count:
2 bread/starch, 1 fat

"Hands on" preparation time: 15 min.
Baking time: 40 min.

Pavlova
Yield: 8 servings

* * *

> 4 large eggs, separated
> 1/4 tsp. salt
> 1/2 c. granulated sugar
> 1/2 c. powdered sugar
> 1 tsp. cornstarch
> 1/2 tsp. vinegar

Preheat oven to 250° F. Separate eggs and pour the egg whites into a large mixing bowl. Add the salt, and then beat on low speed until foamy. Continue beating until soft peaks form. Gradually add the granulated sugar, one tablespoon at a time. Measure the powdered sugar and the cornstarch into a sifter; slowly sift into the egg whites, using a spatula to carefully blend. Finally, fold in the vinegar. Place a piece of wax paper on a cookie sheet. Spread the egg white mixture in a circle on the paper. Build up the meringue to form the sides of a shell. Bake for 1 hour, or until the shell is crisp and just very lightly colored. When the meringue is baked, remove from the oven and cool. Remove the paper from the shell, place the shell on a serving platter and fill with thickened fruit (check index for page number of Fruited Pie Filling) or fruited frozen yogurt.

Calories per serving: 80
Fat: 0 gm. Cholesterol: 0 mg.
Sodium: 92 mg.
For exchange diets, count:
1 1/2 fruit
Nutrient Alert: This recipe is high in sugar and
is not suitable for persons with diabetes.

"Hands on" preparation time: 15 min.
Baking time: 1 hr.

Peach Pudding
Yield: 4 servings

* * *

---

4 peaches or nectarines (may
  use overly ripe or stringy
  peaches)

3/4 c. boiling water

1 pkg. regular or sugar-free
  lemon gelatin mix

1 c. fresh raspberries
  (optional garnish)

Remove pits from the peaches or nectarines. Purée in blender
until smooth. (Go ahead and blend the peeling and all.) Empty
gelatin into a small mixing bowl, and pour boiling water over
gelatin. Stir to dissolve. Stir in blended fruit. Pour into 4
dessert dishes. Chill for 3 hours. Garnish with fresh raspberries.

Calories per serving: 119
Fat: 0 gm. Cholesterol: 0 g.
Sodium: 26 mg.
For exchange diets, count:
2 fruit

"Hands on" preparation time: 10 min.
Chilling time: 3 hrs.

POUND CAKE WITH
APPLE AND ALMOND TOPPING
YIELD: 12 SERVINGS

* * *

19 oz. pkg. 94% fat-free
  yellow cake mix
2 medium cooking apples (I
  prefer Jonathan, or
  Cortland)
1 TB. margarine
1/4 c. brown sugar
2 TB. raisins
2 TB. almonds
1 tsp. almond extract
1/2 tsp. cinnamon

Prepare cake according to package directions and bake in a loaf
pan for 35 to 40 minutes. Meanwhile, wash, peel and slice apples
into a 1-quart microwave dish. Add 2 TB. water and cook on high
power for 5 minutes. Stir in margarine, brown sugar, almonds,
almond extract and cinnamon. Microwave on high power for 2
minutes, or until mixture starts to thicken. Serve sauce over
sliced pound cake.

Calories per serving: 230
Fat: 4 gm. Cholesterol: 0 mg.
Sodium: 314 mg.
For exchange diets, count:
2 bread/starch, 1 fruit

"Hands on" preparation time: 20 min.
Baking time: 35 min.

Pumpkin Pudding with Caramel Topping
Yield: 8 servings, 3/4 cup each

* * *

1/4 c. brown sugar
1 TB. margarine
2 c. skim milk
16 oz. can solid pumpkin
1/2 c. sugar
4 eggs, slightly beaten or 1 c.
   liquid egg substitute
2 TB. vanilla extract
1 1/2 tsp. cinnamon
1/2 tsp. nutmeg
1/4 tsp. ginger

Preheat oven to 350° F. In a small saucepan, combine margarine and brown sugar. Heat over medium flame, stirring until sugar starts to become brittle. Remove from heat and cool, stirring to break up sugar. Combine all other ingredients in a large mixing bowl and beat well. Spray a 2-quart baking dish with nonstick cooking spray and pour pumpkin mixture into dish. Bake for 35 minutes, then sprinkle the top with caramelized brown sugar. Continue baking for 10 to 15 more minutes, or until pudding has set. Cool for at least 30 minutes and serve. This can be made up to 2 days ahead and chilled.

Calories per serving: 170
Fat: 4 gm. Cholesterol: 138 mg. with egg, 3 mg. with substitute
Sodium: 75 mg.
For exchange diets, count:
2 fruit, 1 fat

"Hands on" preparation time: 15 min.
Baking time: 50 min.
Cooling time: 30 min.

RASPBERRY-FILLED CHOCOLATE CAKE
YIELD: 12 SLICES

* * *

19 oz. package 94% fat-free
chocolate cake mix

2 eggs or 1/2 c. liquid egg
substitute

1 1/2 c. water

2/3 c. reduced sugar
raspberry jam (such as
Simply Fruit®)

2 TB. powdered sugar

1/4 c. chopped almonds

Preheat oven to 350° F. Combine cake mix, eggs and water in a
mixing bowl, and beat on high for 2 minutes. Pour batter into a
tube or pan that has been prepared with nonstick cooking spray.
Bake for 35 minutes, or until cake springs back when touched.
Cool for 30 minutes, then remove from pan. Slice cake in half
horizontally and spread jam over bottom layer. Sprinkle nuts
over jam. Replace top. Sprinkle top with powdered sugar. Cut
and serve.

Calories per serving: 211
Fat: 4 gm. Cholesterol: 45 mg. with egg, 0 mg. with substitute
Sodium: 312 mg.
For exchange diets, count:
2 bread/starch, 1 fruit

"Hands on" preparation time: 15 min.
Baking time: 35 min.
Cooling time: 30 min.

Rhubarb Dream Dessert
Yield: 8 servings

* * *

---

4 c. fresh rhubarb, washed
and chopped fine (may
substitute fresh apples,
berries or peaches)

1/3 c. sugar

1/4 c. flour

1/8 tsp. salt

1/2 tsp. cinnamon

1/4 tsp. nutmeg

2 eggs, beaten or 1/2 c. liquid
egg substitute

1 small pkg. sugar-free
strawberry gelatin

Topping:

2 TB. margarine

2 TB. brown sugar

1/3 c. oatmeal

Preheat oven to 350° F. Spray an 8-inch by 8-inch baking dish
with nonstick cooking spray. Place chopped rhubarb in bottom of
dish. Combine all remaining ingredients in a mixing bowl,
blending well. Pour over rhubarb. Mix together topping
ingredients just until crumbly. Sprinkle over rhubarb. Bake for
35 minutes. Serve with low-fat frozen yogurt.

Calories per serving: 137
Fat: 5 gm. Cholesterol: 68 mg. with eggs, 0 mg. with substitute
Sodium: 86 mg.
For exchange diets, count:
1 fruit, 1/2 bread/starch, 1 fat

"Hands on" preparation time: 15 min.
Baking time: 35 min.

SHORTCAKE FOR STRAWBERRIES
YIELD: 12 SLICES

* * *

> 2 (10 oz.) cans refrigerated
> buttermilk biscuits
> 2 TB. melted margarine
> 2/3 c. sugar
> 1 TB. finely grated orange
> peel

Preheat oven to 375° F. Spray a tube pan with nonstick cooking spray. Separate dough into 20 biscuits. Combine sugar and orange peel. Dip each biscuit into melted margarine, then roll in sugar mixture. Place around edges of prepared pan, overlapping edges slightly. Bake at 375° F. for 25 minutes, or until golden brown. Remove from mold immediately. Cool 10 minutes. Cut into slices and top with season's best berries or fresh fruit.

Calories per serving: 131
Fat: 4 gm. Cholesterol: 0 mg.
Sodium: 248 mg.
For exchange diets, count:
1 1/2 bread/starch

"Hands on" preparation time: 10 min.
Baking and cooling time: 35 min.

Snickerdoodles
Yield: 24 cookies

* * *

Recipe courtesy of Jane A. Kulhman, whose kids love these.

> 1 c. brown sugar
> 2 TB. margarine
> 1/2 c. milk
> 1 egg or 1/4 c. liquid egg
>   substitute
> 2 c. flour
> 2 tsp. baking power
> 1/2 c. finely chopped raisins
> Sugar and cinnamon topping

Preheat oven to 375° F. Cream margarine and brown sugar. Beat in egg and milk. Stir together flour and baking powder in a small bowl and add to batter. Fold in raisins. Drop by spoonfuls onto baking sheet. Press down with a glass that has been dipped in a mixture of sugar and cinnamon. Bake for 12 minutes, or until just golden brown. Remove to a cooling rack.

Calories per serving: 97
Fat: 1 gm. Cholesterol: 12 mg. with egg, 0 mg. with substitute
Sodium: 53 mg.
For exchange diets, count:
1 bread/starch, 1/2 fruit

Preparation time: 15 min.
Baking time: 12 min.

Strawberry - Filled Cheesecake
Yield: 8 slices

* * *

> 16 squares graham crackers
> 1 TB. sugar
> 1 TB. margarine, melted
> 3 oz. lemon gelatin
> 1/2 c. boiling water
> 2 TB. lemon juice
> 2 c. low or nonfat cottage
>   cheese
> 2 c. whipped topping
> 2 c. fresh strawberries, cut in
>   half

Preheat oven to 325° F. Crush graham crackers fine, using a
heavy plastic bag and hammer. Pour crumbs into a 9-inch pie
plate and mix with the sugar and melted margarine. Pat crumbs
evenly over bottom and sides of pan. Bake for 15 minutes.
Meanwhile, in a small mixing bowl, dissolve gelatin in the boiling
water. Pour dissolved gelatin into a blender container. Add
lemon juice and process until smooth. Add 1 c. of cottage cheese
and blend until smooth. Add second cup of cottage cheese and
blend again until smooth. Transfer cheese mixture to a large
mixing bowl, then fold in whipped topping. Pour half of mixture
into the prepared pie crust. Place strawberry halves over this
layer. Top with last half of the mixture. Chill at least 2 hours.
Garnish each slice with fresh strawberry.

Calories per serving: 163
Fat: 6 gm. Cholesterol: 20 mg.
Sodium: 328 mg.
For exchange diets, count:
1/2 fruit, 1 fat, 1 skim milk

"Hands on" preparation time: 20 min.
Chilling time: 2 hr.

Zucchini Brownies
Yield: 30 brownies, each 2-inches square

* * *

3 c. peeled and grated
  zucchini
1 1/2 c. sugar
2/3 c. oil
3 c. flour
1/2 tsp. salt
2 tsp. soda
1/3 c. cocoa
3 tsp. vanilla
1/3 c. coconut
1/2 c. chopped almonds

Preheat oven to 350° F. Mix all ingredients together in 2-quart
mixing bowl. Spray an 8-inch by 15-inch pan with nonstick
cooking spray. Spread batter in pan. Bake for 25 minutes, or
until inserted toothpick comes out clean. Dust with powdered
sugar when cooled.

Calories per 1 serving: 137
Fat: 6 gm. Cholesterol: 0 mg.
Sodium: 92 mg.
For exchange diets, count:
1 bread/starch, 1 fat

Nutrient Alert: This recipe contains a large amount of sugar, and is
not recommended for use by persons with diabetes treated with insulin.

"Hands on" preparation time: 15 min.
Baking time: 25 min.

SNACKS

Caramel Corn
YIELD: *6 QUARTS OR 8 SERVINGS, 3 CUPS EACH*

* * *

3 TB. vegetable oil
2/3 c. popcorn
1/4 tsp. salt
1/3 c. honey
3/4 c. brown sugar
2 TB. margarine

Heat oil and popcorn in a skillet or popper until all kernels are popped. Remove from heat. In a microwave-safe bowl, combine salt, honey, brown sugar and margarine. Microwave on high power for 4 minutes, stopping to stir mixture two times. Pour honey mixture over popped corn, stirring to coat evenly. Cool and eat.

Calories per serving: 241
Fat: 7 gm. Cholesterol: 0 mg.
Sodium: 74 mg.
For exchange diets, count:
2 bread/starch, 1/2 fat
Nutrient Alert: This recipe is not suitable for persons with diabetes.

"Hands on" preparation time: 20 min.

Cocktail Crab Dip
Yield: 1 1/2 cups or 6 servings, 1/4 cup each

* * *

1/4 c. toasted almonds
4 oz. light cream cheese (look
  for 50% reduced-fat)
2 TB. minced onion
1 tsp. horseradish
1 tsp. lemon juice
dash of Worcestershire sauce
1/8 tsp. salt
1/8 tsp. pepper
1/4 c. skim milk
4 oz. shredded crab or mock
  crab

Heat oven to 375° F. Spread almonds in a flat pan and place in oven for 10 minutes. Remove when browned. Combine all other ingredients and place in a casserole dish. Place almonds on top. Bake for 20 minutes or until bubbly. Serve with low fat wheat crackers or pretzel chips.

Calories per serving: 115
Fat: 7 gm. Cholesterol: 13 mg.
Sodium: 150 mg.
For exchange diets, count:
1 fat, 1 lean meat

"Hands on" preparation time: 10 min.
Baking time: 20 min.

Fill Your Tank Ice Tea
Yield: 4 servings, 2 cups each

* * *

> 4 tea bags
> 2 qts. boiling water
> 4 sprigs fresh mint
> 6 oz. frozen lemonade
>   concentrate
> 1/4 c. lime juice

Boil water in a 3-quart saucepan. Add tea bags, remove from heat, add mint, and cover. Allow to steep for at least 7 minutes; then remove tea bags and mint. Add frozen lemonade concentrate and lime juice to tea. Pour over ice and enjoy!

Calories per serving: 79
Fat: 0 gm. Cholesterol: 0 g.
Sodium: 6 mg.
For exchange diets, count:
1 1/2 fruit

"Hands on" preparation time: 10 min.

Football Saturday Couch Potatoes

Yield: 4 servings, 2 skins each

* * *

> 4 large baking potatoes
> 1/4 c. picante sauce
> 1 tsp. vegetable oil
> 1 medium onion, chopped
> 1 clove garlic, minced
> 1/2 c. finely chopped lean ham
> 1/2 tsp. oregano
> 1/4 c. picante sauce
> 2 oz. string cheese, pulled into
>   strips

Preheat oven to 400° F. Scrub potatoes and spray with nonstick cooking spray. Place in microwave oven and cook on high power for 6 minutes, turning twice during cooking. Cut cooked potatoes in half lengthwise, scoop pulp out into a bowl and place potatoes skin side down on a baking sheet. Baste potato skins with picante sauce and place in the oven to crisp for 10 minutes. In a skillet, heat vegetable oil and add onion and garlic. Cook onions and garlic for 3 minutes, then stir in ham, oregano, and picante sauce. Cook until thick. Remove potatoes from oven, fill with ham mixture and top with strips of cheese. Return to 400° F. oven for 10 minutes, then serve. Use leftover potato pulp for mashed potatoes the next day.

Calories per serving: 319
Fat: 6 gm. Cholesterol: 27 mg.
Sodium: 168 mg.
For exchange diets, count:
3 bread/starch, 1 lean meat, 1 vegetable

"Hands on" preparation time: 15 min.
Baking time: 25 min.

Friday Night Fondue
Without the Pot
Yield: 4 servings, 3/4 cup each

* * *

---

1 1/2 c. skim milk

1/4 c. flour

4 oz. can green chilies,
  chopped and drained

1 tsp. garlic powder

1 tsp. ground cumin

1/4 tsp. salt

4 oz. part-skim Monterey
  Jack cheese, shredded

4 c. raw vegetables for
  dipping

4 flour tortillas, quartered
  and rolled up

In a 1-quart microwave dish, combine milk and flour; using a whisk to blend. Stir in chilies, garlic powder, cumin and salt. Microwave on high power for 1 minute. Whisk again and microwave for 2 more minutes, until mixture thickens and boils. Stir in shredded cheese. Microwave on 50% power for 1 more minute, stirring to melt the cheese. Use raw vegetables and rolled up tortillas for dippers in chili and cheese fondue.

Calories per serving: 239
Fat: 6 gm. Cholesterol: 19 mg.
Sodium: 468 mg.
For exchange diets, count:
1 bread/starch, 2 vegetable, 2 lean meat
Nutrient Alert: To reduce sodium, omit salt.

"Hands on" preparation time: 10 min.

Hot Berry Wine
Yield: 8 servings, 5 oz. each

* * *

> 2 c. cran-raspberry juice
>   cocktail
> 1/4 c. water
> 1/2 c. sugar
> 2 sticks cinnamon
> 4 whole cloves
> 1 TB. finely shredded lemon
>   peel
> 1 qt. Burgundy wine
> 1/4 c. lemon juice

Bring first six ingredients to a boil in a large pot. Reduce heat and simmer for 10 minutes. Add wine and lemon juice and transfer to a pot, just to keep warm. Be sure not to boil the mixture after wine is added.

Calories per serving: 142
Fat: 0 gm. Cholesterol: 0 mg.
Sodium: 0 mg.
For exchange diets, count:
2 1/2 fruit

Nutrient Alert: Substitute no-alcohol wine for pregnant and nursing women or persons on medications incompatible with alcohol.

"Hands on" preparation time: 10 min.
Heating time: 10 min.

Hot Broccoli Dip
Yield: 8 servings, 3/4 cup each

* * *

> 1 lb. round bread loaf (rye or French work well)
>
> 1/2 c. finely chopped celery
>
> 1/2 c. chopped onion
>
> 1 TB. margarine
>
> 10 oz. container soft cheddar cheese spread (such as Kraft Spreadery®)
>
> 16 oz. pkg. frozen chopped broccoli, thawed and drained
>
> 1/2 tsp. rosemary

Cut top from bread and remove center, leaving 1-inch shell. Cut removed bread into dipping pieces. In a microwave dish, cook celery and onion with margarine on high power for 4 minutes, stopping once to stir. Stir in cheese spread, broccoli and rosemary. Cook on high power for 4 minutes, until cheese is melted. Pour hot dip into bread shell and serve with bread and vegetable dippers.

Calories per serving: 204
Fat: 5 gm. Cholesterol: 6 mg.
Sodium: 368 mg.
For exchange diets, count:
1 lean meat, 2 bread/starch
(Nutrient analysis includes bread.)

"Hands on" preparation time: 15 min.

Pizza Popcorn
YIELD: 4 SERVINGS, 2 CUPS EACH

* * *

1/3 c. popcorn
1 TB. vegetable oil
1/4 c. part-skim shredded
   mozzarella cheese
1 TB. tomato paste
1 TB. Parmesan cheese
1/4 tsp. oregano
1/8 tsp. garlic salt

To make low-fat popcorn in a skillet, combine 1 TB. oil with 1/3 c. corn. Cover and shake over high flame until popping stops. Mix hot popcorn with mozzarella cheese. Combine tomato paste, Parmesan cheese, oregano and garlic salt in a small cup. Toss with popcorn and cheese and serve.

Calories per serving: 133
Fat: 6 gm. Cholesterol: 16 mg.
Sodium: 296 mg.
For exchange diets, count: 1 lean meat, 1 bread/starch

"Hands on" preparation time: 15 min.

Salmon Spread for Crackers
Yield: 2 c. or 8 servings, 1/4 cup each

* * *

15 1/2 oz. can salmon

4 oz. 50% reduced-fat cream cheese

1 TB. minced onion

2 TB. lemon juice

1/4 tsp. salt

2 tsp. Worcestershire sauce

3 TB. ketchup

1 TB. horseradish

2 tsp. dill weed

1/8 tsp. liquid smoke (optional)

Place cream cheese in a mixing bowl and microwave on high power for 30 seconds to soften. Open salmon, drain and remove any bones. Use a fork to flake salmon into cream cheese. Add all remaining ingredients and mix well. Refrigerate. This will keep 3 days. Serve with low-fat crackers or pretzel chips.

Calories per serving: 106
Fat: 5 gm. Cholesterol: 28 mg.
Sodium: 404 mg.
For exchange diets, count:
2 lean meat
Nutrient Alert: To reduce sodium, substitute tomato sauce for ketchup and omit salt.

"Hands on" preparation time: 10 min.

BIBLIOGRAPHY

American Academy of Family Physicians Foundation. *Nutrition Strategies.* 1990.

American Diabetes Association, Inc. The American Dietetic Association, Inc. *Exchange Lists for Meal Planning.* 1989.

American Heart Association. *An Eating Plan for Healthy Americans.* 1985.

American Institute for Cancer Research. *Dietary Guidelines to Lower Cancer Risk.* 1990.

Anderson, Jean. *The New Doubleday Cookbook.* Garden City, New York: Doubleday and Company. 1985. pp. 28 - 30.

Food Service. "National Study: Latest Stats Support 'Light' Eating Trends" Calorie Control Council. Booth Research Service. July 15, 1991.

Garner, Peter. "Most Potent Anti-aging Tool Begins to Yield Secrets." *Chicago Tribune.* December 12, 1991.

General Mills. *The American Breakfast Report: A 10-Year Survey of 4000 Households.* 1991.

Streit, Kelly. "Food Records: A Predictor of and Modifier of Weight Change in a Long-term Weight Loss Program." *Journal of the American Dietetic Association.* 1991. Vol. 91, p. 213.

USDA and USDHHS: *Dietary Guidelines for Americans,* 1990.

INDEX

CHRONIMED Publishing Books of Related Interest

Let Them Eat Cake by Virginia N. White with Rosa A. Mo, R.D. If you're looking for delicious and healthy pies, cookies, puddings, and cakes, this book will give you your just desserts. With easy, step-by-step instructions, this innovative cookbook features complete nutrition information, the latest exchange values, and tips on making your favorite snacks more healthful.

004206, ISBN 1-56561-011-3 $12.95

All-American Low-Fat Meals in Minutes by M.J. Smith, R.D., L.D., M.A. Filled with tantalizing recipes and valuable tips, this cookbook makes great-tasting low-fat foods a snap for holidays, special occasions, or everyday. Most recipes take only minutes to prepare.

004079, ISBN 0-937721-73-5 $12.95

The Guiltless Gourmet by Judy Gilliard and Joy Kirkpatrick, R.D. A perfect fusion of sound nutrition and creative cooking, this book is loaded with delicious recipes high in flavor and low in fat, sugar, calories, cholesterol, and salt.

004021, ISBN 0-937721-23-9 $9.95

The Guiltless Gourmet Goes Ethnic by Judy Gilliard and Joy Kirkpatrick, R.D. More than a cookbook, this sequel to *The Guiltless Gourmet* shows how easy it is to lower the sugar, calories, sodium, and fat in your favorite ethnic dishes—without sacrificing taste.

004072, ISBN 0-937721-68-9 $11.95

European Cuisine from the Guiltless Gourmet by Judy Gilliard and Joy Kirkpatrick, R.D. This book shows you how to lower the sugar, salt, cholesterol, total fat, and calories in delicious Greek, English, German, Russian, and Scandinavian dishes. Plus it features complete nutrition information and the latest exchange values.

004085, ISBN 0-937721-81-6 $11.95

The Joy of Snacks by Nancy Cooper, R.D. Offers more than 200 delicious recipes and nutrition information for hearty snacks, including sandwiches, appetizers, soups, spreads, cookies, muffins, and treats especially for kids. The book also suggests guidelines for selecting convenience snacks and interpreting information on food labels.

004086, ISBN 0-937721-82-4 $12.95

Convenience Food Facts by Marion Franz, R.D., M.S., and Arlene Monk, R.D., C.D.E. Includes complete nutrition information, tips, and exchange values on more than 1,500 popular name-brand processed foods commonly found in grocery store freezers and shelves. Helps you plan easy-to-prepare, nutritious meals.

004081, ISBN 0-937721-77-8 $10.95

Fast Food Facts by Marion Franz, R.D., M.S. This revised and up-to-date best-seller shows how to make smart nutrition choices at fast food restaurants—and tells what to avoid. Includes complete nutrition information on more than 1,000 menu offerings from the 21 largest fast food chains.

Standard-size edition   004068, ISBN 0-937721-67-0 $6.95
Pocket edition   004073, ISBN 0-937721-69-7 $4.95

Exchanges for All Occasions by Marion Franz, R.D., M.S. Exchanges and meal planning suggestions for just about any occasion, sample meal plans, special tips for people with diabetes, and more.

004003, ISBN 0-937721-22-0 $8.95